The IMC PlanPro Handbook

The IMC PlanPro Handbook

Kenneth E. Clow | **Donald Baack**
University of Louisiana at Monroe Pittsburgh State University

Upper Saddle River, New Jersey 07458

VP/Editorial Director: Jeff Shelstad
Acquisitions Editor: Katie Stevens
Project Development Manager: Ashley Santora
Associate Director Manufacturing: Vincent Scelta
Production Editor & Buyer: Wanda Rockwell
Printer/Binder: Bind-Rite Graphics

Copyright © 2007 by Pearson Education, Inc., Upper Saddle River, New Jersey, 07458.
Pearson Prentice Hall. All rights reserved. Printed in the United States of America. This publication is protected by Copyright and permission should be obtained from the publisher prior to any prohibited reproduction, storage in a retrieval system, or transmission in any form or by any means, electronic, mechanical, photocopying, recording, or likewise. For information regarding permission(s), write to: Rights and Permissions Department.

Pearson Prentice Hall™ is a trademark of Pearson Education, Inc.

10 9 8 7 6 5 4 3 2 1
ISBN 0-13-186630-3

Contents

Building an IMC Plan 1

Section 1: Executive Summary 9

Section 2: Promotions Opportunity Analysis 11

Section 3: Corporate Strategies 39

Section 4: IMC Management 67

Section 5: IMC Objective One: Consumers 87

Section 6: IMC Objective Two: Distribution Channel 125

Section 7: IMC Objective Three: Business-to-Business 149

Section 8: Samples 173

To my sons Dallas, Wes, Tim, and Roy who provided encouragement and especially to my wife, Susan,

whose sacrifice and love made this textbook possible.

*— **Kenneth E. Clow***

I would like to dedicate my efforts and contributions to the book to my wife Pam, children, Jessica,

Daniel, and David, and grandchildren, Danielle, Rile and Andrew.

*— **Donald Baack***

Preface

We created *IMC Plan Pro Booklet* to support our *Integrated Advertising, Promotions, and Marketing Communications* text, for instructors who like to assign a semester long project and challenge students to apply the information contained in our IMC textbook. While this booklet can be used in conjunction with our textbook, it can also be used as a stand-alone supplement to other textbooks or the primary instructional material for an applied course in Integrated Marketing Communication design.

With this IMC Plan Pro Booklet and software, students are able create their on integrated marketing communications plans, complete with sample ads and related marketing materials. The software allows students to modify the outline of the program to fit their particular product or their particular IMC Plan. With this application booklet and project, students will gain a first-hand experience about how to completely integrate a marketing plan, from the beginning to end.

The software allows students to spend more time on developing the actual IMC plan and less time on formatting pages, inserting tables, and building graphs. The software does all of this for the student once the data have been entered.

Acknowledgments

We would like to thank the following individuals who assisted in the development of this text. We very much appreciate Wil Mara and Katie Stevens are our current editors for giving us the opportunity to write this text and for their insightful opinions and quality advice. We would also like to thank the entire Prentice Hall production team.

Kenneth Clow would like to thank the University of Louisiana at Monroe for providing a supporting environment to work on this text. He is thankful to his sons Dallas, Wes, Tim, and Roy who always provided encouragement and support.

Donald Baack would like to thank Mimi Morrison for her continual assistance in all his work at Pittsburg State University. Christine Fogliasso has been a great help in her role as department chairperson. She helped make his workload manageable during the preparation of the manuscript. Also, Dr. Jerry Rogers has offered advice regarding this disk and other IMC materials over the past several years.

We would like to especially thank our wives, Susan Clow and Pam Baack, for being patient and supportive during those times when we were swamped by the work involved in completing this edition. They have been enthusiastic and understanding throughout this entire journey.

Building an IMC Plan

Building an IMC Plan takes thought, planning, and hard work. This booklet and the accompanying IMC Plan Pro Software make developing an IMC Plan much easier. An outline is already developed for you. Instructions and samples are provided for each section of the IMC plan. These features will guide you as your prepare the information to be placed in your individual IMC Plan. Also, tables have already been placed in strategic locations throughout the software. All you have to do is supply the data that is requested. Once entered, the software automatically generates accompanying graphs that visually illustrate the data. By following the instructions in this booklet and by examining the sample plan provided, you will be able develop a concise, professional IMC Plan.

This booklet is organized to match the IMC Plan Pro software. The booklet is divided into 8 sections that correspond with each section on the IMC Plan Pro software. Within each section in this booklet, a brief overview is provided along with an explanation of the concepts that are involved. Next, instructions about how to complete each part of the IMC Plan within that section are presented. In addition, a sample from the IMC Plan Pro software is provided in the text so you can see one example of that particular section. For most of the samples, Willamette Furniture is used. This sample IMC Plan was selected because of its comprehensive nature and applicability to the various sections of the IMC Plan.

Several options can be used in developing the IMC Plan. Of course, the first option is to begin with the first section of this booklet and the IMC Plan and proceed to the last section. This works well if this booklet is being used as a stand-alone course, an independent project within a college course, or for someone developing a personal IMC Plan for some other purpose.

The second option is to use this software with the *Integrated Advertising, Promotions, and Marketing Communications,* 3rd edition textbook by Clow and Baack, published by Prentice-Hall. For this option, the appendix contains a useful outline indicating the sections of the IMC Plan that are associated with each chapter of the textbook. This will allow for immediate application of the concepts and theories presented in individual chapters. While this method has you moving around in the software to complete various sections, it does provide for reinforcement of the concepts in the textbook and allows you to integrate textbook learning with practical application.

The third option occurs when this *IMC Plan Pro Booklet* is being used with another textbook. In this situation, various sections of the IMC Plan can be completed as they correspond to the textbook being used. As an alternative, the IMC Plan can be completed independent of the textbook. If you have taken courses in marketing, you should be able to complete this IMC Plan without any additional textbook. The instructions and samples that are presented in each section of the IMC Plan are phrased in terms that are familiar to those with a marketing background.

Using the IMC Plan Pro Software

The IMC Plan Pro Software was developed to provide an easy-to-use template to create an Integrated Marketing Communications Plan. To use the IMC Plan Pro software, you must have Adobe Acrobat Reader on your computer, preferably the latest version. If you do not, a free version can be obtained by accessing the Adobe web site at http://www.adobe.com.

To download the IMC Plan Pro Software, follow the instructions on the disk as well as what appears on the screen once the disk is placed in your CD-ROM drive. If you receive an error message in the downloading process that you do not have the latest version of Adobe Acrobat Reader, remove the disk and download the latest version. If after the latest version of Adobe Reader is downloaded and you still receive an error message concerning the Adobe Reader, you will need to access the web site of the IMC Plan Pro developer, Palo Alto Software, to download a patch. This can be obtained through tech support at http://www.paloalto.com.

After the software is downloaded on your hard drive, be sure to access the software. The first time you do so, it will ask for the serial number that is packaged with the disk. While this serial number is not needed to download the software, it is needed to access the software. You are now ready to develop your IMC Plan.

To use the software it is helpful to access one of the sample IMC Plans provided. Each one provides the opportunity to review a completed IMC Plan. To access sample plans, click on the "Sample Plans" button along the top menu of your screen. A window will open with several sample plans (see the screen capture below). Click on the one you want to see. It will open in a separate window in Acrobat Reader. You can either scroll through the samples on the screen or print them off to refer to as you develop your plan.

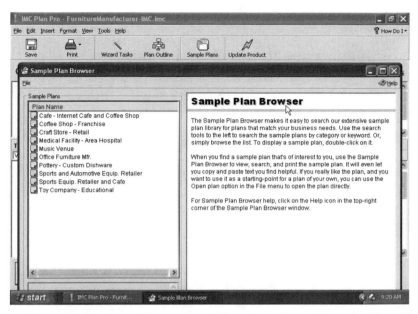

Figure 0.1 — The IMC Plan Pro Software provides a number of sample plans that you can examine and print.

Once you have an idea of what the IMC Plan will look like, you are ready to begin. Access the "Plan Setup" from the "File" menu on your screen. Instructions are provided in the instruction box located near the top of the screen just below the menu bar. Once you have completed the task that is explained, use the "Next Task" button on the screen to go to the next part of the setup process. After completing the IMC Plan setup, you are ready to begin.

The "Wizard Task" button on the top menu is useful for easy access to different components of the plan. When you click on it, the outline of an IMC Plan appears in a window along the left side of the screen. You can access any segment of the IMC Plan by just clicking on the menu item. For example, in the screen capture below, the Promotion Opportunity Analysis portion of an IMC Plan for Willamette Furniture is shown. Notice in the bottom portion of the screen is the actual Willamette IMC Plan. This are is where you will be inputting information for your plan. Above the input area are the instructions on what is to be contained in that particular section. If you are unclear about what should be in the section after reading the instructions, notice that to the right of the instructions is a box with the word "Examples" in it. If you click on this link, one or two different examples will appear so you can see how this section was written in other IMC Plans.

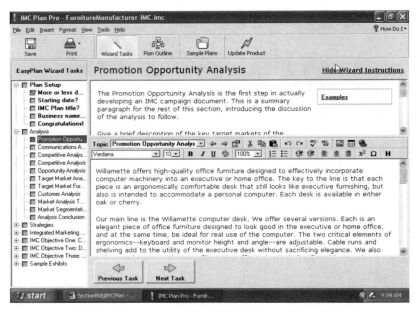

Figure 0.2 — The IMC Plan Pro software provides instructions and examples for each section of the plan to guide you in developing your plan.

The "Plan Outline" button on the top menu provides the outline of your IMC Plan along the left side of your screen. In Figure 0.3, is the "Target Markets" pie chart that is found in Section 2.2 of the Willamette Furniture IMC Plan. This pie chart was produced when the authors of the Willamette Furniture plan inserted the data in the table provided in the software. This plan outline can be used to quickly move to any portion of the IMC Plan and to view graphs and charts that have been created.

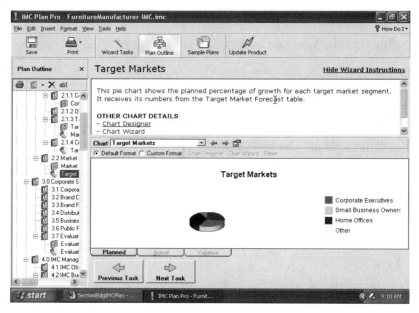

Figure 0.3 — The plan outline button is useful for navigating to various sections of the plan.

The Printing Function

The printing function allows you to print all or part of your IMC Plan as well as view all or specific components of the IMC Plan. Notice the print options menu in the screen capture below. The various components of the plan that are checked indicate these components will be printed unless you remove the check mark. You do not have to build the "Table of Contents," the software automatically does this for you. Unless you uncheck a box when you print the complete IMC Plan, the printed plan will include the Table of Contents, the legal page, the cover page, appendices, tables, and charts. Also included under the print options menu are settings for headers and footers, font settings, and margins. Any of these can be modified.

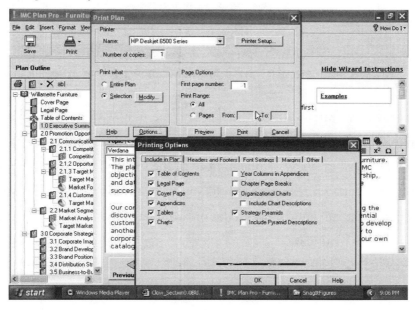

Figure 0.4 — The print options menu allows you to modify what and how the IMC Plan will be printed.

In working with your IMC Plan, you may want to print a section or specific sections to see what the plan looks like rather than the entire plan. By using the "Selection" menu under "Print what" you can do this. When you access the "Selection" by clicking on the "Modify" button, another screen will appear. You can select a particular section you want to print or various sections you want to see.

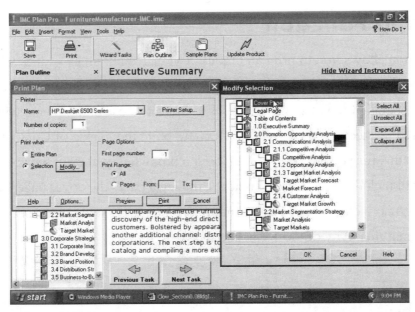

Figure 0.5 — The IMC Plan Pro software print menu allows you to print the entire plan or only specific sections.

You may not want to print your IMC Plan, but you may want to preview it so you can see what it will look like. This can be done through the print menu. After accessing the print menu, click on the button that says "Preview" at the bottom of the menu. The IMC Plan Pro software will produce your plan in a separate screen as it would appear if it is printed. By using the buttons on the top of the menu, you can advance through the preview page by page. You can also enlarge the preview to the full screen if you want.

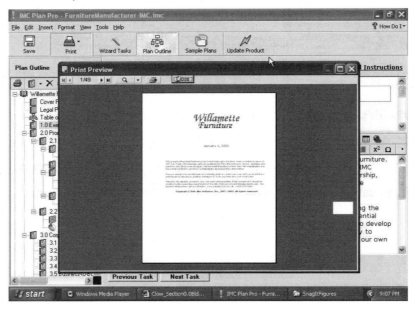

Figure 0.6 — Through the print menu, the IMC Plan Pro software allows you to preview your plan at anytime.

In addition to printing and previewing your IMC Plan, you can examine specific reports by accessing the "Reports" menu when you first access the "Print" button on the top of your menu bar. Reports include your tables and charts that are currently in your outline. By going to the bottom of the menu, you have the option to either print or preview your tables and charts. This is a helpful function when you are entering your data and you want to take a look at how the table and/or chart will appear but are not interested in seeing the IMC Plan itself.

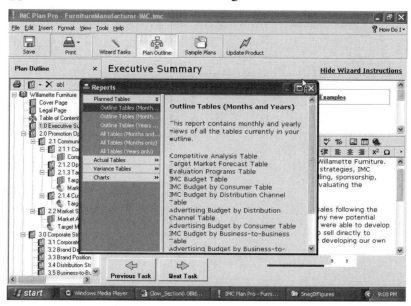

Figure 0.7 — The reports section of the print menu allows you to examine the tables and charts that are part of your IMC Plan outline.

Section 1
Executive Summary

Most executives are busy people. They require information that is summarized and easy to read. The goal is to save time and pay attention to the most important tasks and facts. The IMC Plan Pro disk begins with a section called "Executive Summary." It is designed to reveal the key points and facts about your IMC plan.

Section 1.0

Although this section appears first in the plan outline, it probably a good idea to write it last. You won't know all of the contents of this section until the rest of your IMC plan has been developed. When you finally write the Executive Summary, be sure it includes overview of your target markets, corporate strategies, Integrated Marketing Communications (IMC) management issues, budget and methodologies. The summary should old provide an outline the three IMC communications objectives and the corporate and brand-image strategy that were developed within the plan.

An ideal Executive Summary is written in such a manner that if it was the only part of the plan that was read by a corporate executive, the executive would have a very good idea about what the plan contains. The executive should be able to walk away after reading the summary thinking "I know what is being planned." Later when as the rest of the plan unfolds, your executive officer will exclaim, "This is a great IMC Plan! It is clear, concise, and readable. I like it!"

1.0 Executive Summary

This integrated marketing communications plan is designed for Willamette Furniture. The plan includes a promotions opportunity analysis, corporate strategies, IMC objectives, plus all relevant advertising, promotion, personal selling, sponsorship, and database programs. Finally, a media plan and methods of evaluating the success of the IMC plan are described.

Our company, Willamette Furniture experienced an increase in sales following the discovery of the high-end direct mail channel that identified many new potential customers. Bolstered by appearances in specialty catalogs, we were able to develop another additional channel: distributors of office equipment who sell directly to corporations. The next step is to move into direct marketing by developing our own catalog and compiling a more extensive database.

By targeting the high-end market, we can successfully occupy an emerging niche that other channels of distribution have not targeted. The implementation of the new integrated marketing focus, as outlined in this plan, positions our product line as the high-quality, elegant alternative to mainstream office furniture that is typically found in office supply stores. Our ability to integrate emerging technologies in a design, provide complimentary pieces for a complete set, and custom design ergonomic executive-level office furniture, will help us establish a reputation of unmatched quality.

While continuing to serve the corporate executive, we will aggressively seek the home office market segment. This segment is projected to be the fastest growing portion of our business over the next five years. The goal is to develop an integrated marketing communications program that includes advertising, promotions, sponsorships and direct marketing, in order to increase the share of each of the markets we serve, with the highest growth being in the home office segment.

Section 2
Promotions Opportunity Analysis

The first step in creating an effective Integrated Marketing Communications program is to identify all target markets for the company's products. The tool you will use is called a promotions opportunity analysis. Besides discovering the target audiences for various products, it is important to find the best methods for reaching each individual target market.

Individual consumer groups use products in different ways. Think about an item as simple as orange juice. Some consumers have it with breakfast. Others mix it with vodka to make a screwdriver. Others still use orange juice as an afternoon drink for their children, instead of a soft drink such as Pepsi or Coke. Each group may want a different size package and may view the product in distinct ways.

The same pattern holds true for products sold to businesses. These differences are especially noticeable in global markets. Consequently, marketing messages that are targeted to various types of customers requires separate and somewhat customized approaches. An effective promotional analysis identifies the best approach or appeal for each set of customers.

Two primary objectives are included in a promotions opportunity analysis. The first is to determine which promotional opportunities exist for the company. This means looking for sets of consumers or businesses that can be viewed as viable target markets.

The second objective is to identify the characteristics of each target audience. The ultimate goal is to reach each group with effective advertising and marketing communications messages. The more you understand about an audience, the greater the chance a message will be heard, understood, and result in the desired outcome, such as improved brand awareness, more frequent purchases, or increased brand loyalty.

Completing a promotions opportunity analysis includes two components: (1) a communication analysis and (2) a market segmentation strategy. Remember that these two activities are closely associated with each other.

The first activity is a **communication analysis**. It is covered in part 2.1 on your IMC Plan Pro disk. A communication analysis begins with an examination of the various types of communications used in the industry. There are four steps: (1) a competitive analysis, (2) an opportunity analysis, (3) a target market analysis, and (4) a customer analysis. These steps are listed as 2.1.1, 2.1.2, 2.1.3, and 2.1.4 on your disk. Examples of each are also provided.

11

A *competitive analysis* is the study of your company's primary competitors and the types of communication strategies each uses. Within the same industry, some competitors may focus on informative messages, others on emotional appeals, and others may emphasize price. In the car insurance industry, these three strategies are easy to spot when watching or hearing individual advertisements.

An *opportunity analysis* examines the opportunities that exist for your product. For instance, a product that is superior may feature an opportunity to promote quality. A service provider may be able to emphasize location and convenience. The idea is to match the needs of a consumer group with one of these product features or advantages.

A *target market analysis* describes the various target markets that would be viable customers for each product. In the case of auto insurance, one set of customers is teenagers and other higher-risk drivers. A second set would be mature and experienced drivers. Other groups may consist of families that own more than one car or consumers that wish to have all of their insurance needs met by a single company.

A *customer analysis* is the final component of the communications analysis. The goal is to provide a detailed description of the typical customers of your products. The typical customers for Allstate Insurance may be those who want high quality service when an accident occurs. The typical customers for Geico insurance may be those looking for a lower price.

A **market segmentation analysis** is the second component of a promotions opportunity analysis. The analysis should be designed to identify the method of segmentation that will be used and the various target markets to be pursued. This activity is covered in section 2.2 on your disk. With this information, you will be prepared to make solid decisions while developing the rest of your IMC Plan.

Section 2.0

The opening part of Section 2.0 of the IMC plan that you are writing should contain a brief background for the corporate executive or reader of the plan. This background includes a description of the corporation and its history, especially as it relates to the product that is the subject of your IMC plan. Remember to mention any other products the corporation sells and how each product or brand fits into the company's product mix.

The second element in this section is a brief overview of the company's marketing plan. This includes a review of the marketing mix variables, which are product, price, promotion, and distribution. Describing the product to be marketed is the first step. The description includes the unique features that will be highlighted in your IMC plan.

Next, the IMC plan should discuss the company's pricing strategy. The presentation will be fairly general, using terms like "high end" or "lowest price." It is not important to mention specific prices.

Third, an overview of promotions should be provided. If the company sells other products, describe how this IMC plan will dovetail with the promotions developed for the company's other products as well as with the company as a whole.

The fourth part is to explain the distribution strategy that will be used to market this product. This information is valuable as it sets the stage upon which the IMC plan will be built.

A promotions opportunity analysis for the Willamette Furniture company is shown below. It should give you a general idea about how to prepare the analysis for your own IMC plan.

2.0 Promotion Opportunity Analysis

Willamette Furniture has been manufacturing office furniture for over 20 years. The company has grown from initial sales of $32,000 the first year to $87 million in 2004. Willamette offers high-quality office furniture designed to effectively incorporate computers into an executive or home office. The key to the line is that each piece is an ergonomically comfortable desk that still looks like executive furnishing, but also accommodates a personal computer. Each desk is available in either oak or cherry.

Our primary marketing strategy is to be certain that the right information is available to the right target customer. We must make sure our resources are used to sell products to individuals and companies with sufficient funds to acquire higher priced items. The objective is make sure that those who have the budget and appreciate these products will know that they exist and how to find them.

The IMC program must convey a sense of quality in every picture, promotion, and publication. Willamette cannot afford a second-rate appearance in any marketing piece or advertisement. Poor illustrations or low-quality promotions will that make our products look less elegant. It is crucial to effectively enhance our appearance using high-quality catalogs and specialty distributors.

Our main **product** line is the Willamette computer desk. We offer several versions. Each is an elegant piece of office furniture designed to look good in the executive or home office, and at the same time, be ideal for real use of the computer. The two critical elements of ergonomics--keyboard and monitor height and angle--are adjustable. Cable runs and shelving add to the utility of the executive desk without sacrificing elegance. We also make complementary pieces to fill out an office suite, including file cabinets, printer stands, and bookcases.

We also create custom designs to fit exact measurements. Further supporting this competitive edge is our assembly strategy, which is based on interlocking wood pieces of such high quality that assembly is simple and enjoyable. This feature enhances the sense of quality associated with each product.

In the coming year a new custom option to the executive desk line will be introduced. It will accommodate a laptop computer with a docking station to connect to a network. The new desk is designed to easy access to the docking station. This allows for better use of the space because it doesn't have to be dedicated to a CPU case.

The furniture also accommodates larger computer monitors, including the 17", 19", and 21" sizes that are becoming much more common, particularly in the high-end market. We will monitor other technological developments, allowing Willamette to be the first to provide custom furniture for wall-mounted flat screens, liquid crystal displays, and similar innovations as they become available.

Our **pricing** strategy is at the high end of the furniture industry. This matches with a heavy emphasis on the quality of our merchandise. It also means mass marketing efforts are not viable.

Our **distribution** strategy is to reach customers who are seeking quality office furniture with specific technological needs. Our retail and business to business operations marketing programs are aimed currently through high-level retail stores such as Sharper

> Image. We will also feature internal catalog publishing to our existing catalog. Since our products are connected to the use of computer technology, the development of a Willamette website will increase the company's profile by promoting the product line in a medium that is most appropriate to our customers.
>
> Willamette Furniture's **promotions** are focused on executive level customers who have an appreciation for quality craftsmanship and materials. These individuals will buy products that integrate technology into an office environment. Primary customers for office furniture include corporate executives, small business owners, and home office users. They will be reached through a variety of media, including the Internet, catalogs, personal selling approaches, selective advertising, and various channel promotions.

Section 2.1   Communications Analysis

As you write the IMC plan, section 2.1 will help you identify and analyze the communications in your industry as well as the marketing environment in which your company operates. This is not a SWOT (strengths, weaknesses, opportunities, threats) analysis, which should have been conducted in developing the marketing plan. Instead, you will examine the communication aspects of your competitors, target market, and customers.

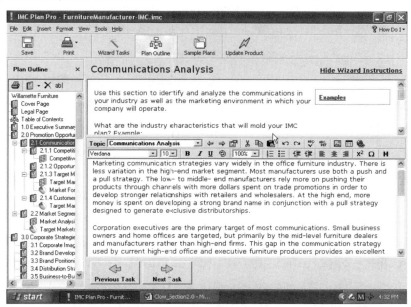

Figure 2.1 — The Communications Analysis is in Section 2.1 of the IMC Plan Pro software.

In the first part of 2.1 in your IMC Plan, note the overall communication strategies used in the industry. For instance, do most companies in the industry use television advertising supplemented with print ads or is print used primarily? What about the use of consumer and trade promotions? What about the use of sponsorships and personal selling? Remember to consider the business-to-business markets as well as the consumer markets. As the communications analysis unfolds, you will individually discuss each of its four parts, the competitive analysis, opportunity analysis, target market analysis, and customer analysis.

Here is an example of a communications analysis as it applies to Willamette Furniture.

2.1 Communications Analysis

Marketing communication strategies vary widely in the office furniture industry. There is less variation in the high-end market segment. Most manufacturers use both a push and a pull strategy. The low- to middle- end manufacturers rely more on pushing their products through channels with more dollars spent on trade promotions in order to develop stronger relationships with retailers and wholesalers. At the high end, more money is spent on developing a strong brand name in conjunction with a pull strategy designed to generate exclusive distributorships.

Corporate executives are the primary targets of most communications. Small business owners and home offices are also targeted, but primarily by the mid-level furniture dealers and manufacturers rather than by high-end firms. This gap in the communication strategy used by current high-end office and executive furniture producers provides an excellent communication opportunity for Willamette Furniture.

In examining the communication strategies of the high-end office furniture manufacturers and dealers, the following facts were discovered:

1) Home offices and small business owners are not a high target priority of the current firms in the industry.

2) Personal selling is the primary communication strategy for the high-end firms who are targeting corporate executives.

3) Furniture dealers, such as Rocky Mountain Desk Corporation, are the major distribution outlets for high-end manufacturers. Manufacturers rely heavily on trade promotions with these furniture dealers to push products.

4) Direct marketing is used by some firms, but not extensively. As with Willamette, catalogs are the primary direct marketing tool being used.

5) The Internet is rapidly becoming a major source of information and purchasing for small business owners and home offices. Most high-end firms have not effectively used the Internet as a means of selling products. Instead, the Internet is most often used to provide information and to obtain prospect names for subsequent personal sales calls or telemarketing contacts.

Section 2.1.1 Competitive Analysis

The objective of a competitive analysis is to identify your major competitors and to examine the communication strategies each uses to reach customers. The analysis should reveal the individual types or groups of competitors you face. For example, if Willamette designs an IMC program aimed at the upper end of the office furniture market, then in the competitive analysis Willamette would need to know which other firms target these upper end customers. A company that establishes a marketing program aimed at the low end office furniture market has a different set of competitors. While there may be some overlap of competitors in the two markets, both should have a clear idea of their particular markets when this activity is completed. The same approach would be used for international markets, even though competitors could be domestic or global companies.

To complete section 2.1.1, you need to identify who the competition is and what they are doing in the areas of advertising and communication. This is important because consumers mentally integrate information from a variety of sources. As a result, it is necessary to find out as much as possible about the things potential customers are seeing, hearing, and reading about the competition.

Once the major categories of competitors have been identified, you are ready to investigate actual competitors. Choose the main companies or brands that offer the most direct and challenging competition. These should be listed in the first row of the Competitive Analysis Table in this section of the IMC Plan Pro.

As an example, review the plan for Kaolin Calefactors that is on your IMC Plan Pro disk. Kaolin designs and manufactures custom dishware. The company competes with firms in three different types of industries: commercial dishware manufactures, assorted craftspeople, and other potters. Since Kaolin manufactures dishware, one competitor is mass manufactures, such as Lenox. Kaolin also competes with craftspeople that design and produce custom-made dishware, such as LDA Creations and Cridge, Inc. Kaolin's most direct competitor are other potters who design individualized dishware. The most intense competitors from this group are NCM Studies, Inc. and Midwest Pottery.

In developing Kaolin's list of competitors, the marketing team discovered that while other potters are the primary competitors, consumers do have additional choices. They can purchase dishware at retail outlets for mass manufacturers. While these are not customized or unique designs, they offer alternatives that consumers might consider while making purchase decisions. Also, some consumers purchase dishware from craftspeople. This market segment, however, tends to make purchases of dishware for gifts rather than for personal use.

As part of preparing section 2.1.1, fill in the first column of the Competitive Analysis Table. List the criteria that will be used for the competitive analysis. These should be customized to fit your industry. For instance, for Willamette Furniture, the primary categories are the product and/or service, distribution channel, added value factors, and communication analysis. This last category is very important. Typical factors to consider include:

- Advertising
- Trade promotions
- Consumer promotions
- Personal selling
- Database marketing programs
- E-commerce or web sites
- Sponsorships and event marketing
- Direct market programs
- Public relations

Look closely at how each competitor identifies markets their particular brands. Ask key questions, including the following: Do they use advertising? If so, where and when do they advertise? What is the quality of their advertising? Is it effective? Does it stand out, and, if so, how? Do consumers readily identify the ads and relate to them? The same type of questions should be asked about each type of communication that is being analyzed. The goal of this analysis is to understand how the competition is communicating to consumers and what your company needs to do to effectively compete.

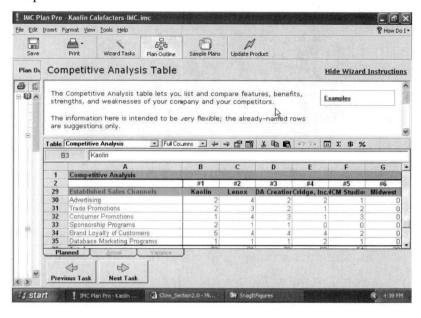

Figure 2.2 — The competitive analysis for Kaolin involves evaluating each competitor on a number of criteria, such as advertising, trade promotions, and consumer promotions.

After completing a list of primary competing firms and the criteria that will be used in the analysis, the company can continue a competitive analysis by collecting secondary data. The first items to look for are statements competitors make about themselves. Sources of secondary data about competitors can be found in:

- Advertisements
- Promotional materials
- Annual reports
- A prospectus for a publicly held corporation
- Web sites

The idea is to obtain as much information as you can about the competition. In this case, you should be especially interested in what they say to customers.

The next task is to study what *other people* are saying about the competition. This information can be gathered from several sources. You will need to examine trade journals and visit with vendors and suppliers. They may have dealt with the competition or have read the competition's literature. The library may also yield news articles and press releases regarding competitor activities. The goal is to find out how other companies close to the competition view them. This information provides a sense of how to view each company in comparison with the competition.

2.1.1 Competitive Analysis

Willamette Furniture occupies a specific niche within the office furniture market. Few competitors provide comparable products. They do not utilize our unique combination of technological integration, quality materials, and craftsmanship. Our strongest competition includes Ethan Allen, Acme Computer Furniture, Neville Johnson and ABCO Office Manufacturing. These companies distribute products through channels such as chain office supply stores, furniture dealers, or company-owned retail locations. In contrast, Willamette targets potential customers who are already searching for high-quality office products. The following is a review of Willamette Furniture's primary competitors.

Ethan Allen has been in business since 1932. The company is a major player in the high-end office furniture market. In addition to 20 manufacturing facilities, the company owns 11 distribution facilities and 310 retail outlets. The firm's large size, high exposure, and high-quality furniture makes Ethan Allen a competitor for facilities furniture. In addition to company stores, Ethan Allen utilizes a direct marketing catalog program and is also developing a presence in online markets. The company's direct marketing catalog is aimed almost entirely at large businesses and customers of the firm's retail operation. The company does not aggressively seek small businesses and home office users. The goal of both Ethan Allen's catalog program and direct marketing program is to draw business into retail stores. Ethan Allen is vertically integrated, from saw mills through to retail operations. This means the company poses the most serious challenge to Willamette Furniture, primarily because of their operational economies-of-scales.

Acme Computer Furniture has been in business since 1985. Acme specializes in oak furniture. Acme markets through furniture distributors, dealers, and retailers. The company does not have its own sales force and does not sell directly to any type of customer.

Instead, Acme uses manufacturers' reps. The company does maintain a website, but only for the purpose of providing information to customers. The furniture is of excellent quality, however, due to the margins charged by the various middlemen, Willamette should able to beat Acme's prices in most cases. Acme Computer's marketing dollars go primarily to trade promotions with some advertising in trade and furniture catalogs.

Neville Johnson has been in business only 13 years. The company specializes in custom-made, custom-installed office furniture. Neville carries a staff of designers and installers. Its market is almost exclusively corporate executives and large businesses. Few small businesses or home office users can afford Neville Johnson's products, because of the firm's custom design process. Neville sells through distributorships but also maintains a direct sales force and a direct marketing program to garner most sales. Willamette should be able to compete with Neville because we offer almost the same types of furniture, pre-made, which means the design fees are saved. Neville Johnson's competitive advantage is with Fortune 500 companies.

At the retail level, Office Max, Office Depot, and Staples are also competitors. Small businesses and home office users are attracted to these retail outlets. Attractive prices, easy accessibility, and variety are desirable for business customers who may prefer higher-end furniture but may opt out in favor of lower priced, lower grade alternative. While these retail stores do compete against Willamette, they are not major competitors because of our philosophy and image. Willamette's goal is to provide information to individuals who desire high-quality furniture but are not as yet aware of what we offer.

The following table is a competitive analysis of our five major competitors. A score of "5" indicates excellent or good while a score of "1" indicates poor or inadequate.

Competitive Analysis	#1	#2	#3	#4	#5	#6
Competitors	Acme	ABCO	Ethan Allen	Neville Johnso	Office Depot	Staples
Quality	3	3	5	5	2	2
Ergonomic design	3	3	4	5	1	1
Craftsmanship	3	3	5	5	3	2
Selection	4	3	5	4	4	3
Price	4	4	3	3	5	4
Distribution Channel	Acme	ABCO	Ethan Allen	Neville Johnso	Office Depot	Staples
Number of distributors	4	4	2	3	5	5
Relationships with	3	4	3	5	4	4
Direct marketing of	2	2	2	1	1	1
Use of trade incentives	5	5	2	2	0	0

Added Value Factors	Acme	ABCO	Ethan Allen	Neville Johnso	Office Depot	Staples
Pre and Post Sales Service	4	3	5	3	2	2
Experience	4	4	5	4	2	3
Expertise	4	3	5	3	3	2
Reputation	4	4	5	3	3	3
Image	4	3	5	3	3	3
Strategic Alliances	3	2	4	3	3	2
Other	4	3	5	4	4	4

Communication Analysis	Acme	ABCO	Ethan Allen	Neville Johnso	Office Depot	Staples
Advertising	3	3	5	3	5	5
Database programs	2	2	3	2	2	3
Web site	3	3	4	2	4	4
Trade promotions	4	4	3	4	2	3
Consumer promotions	3	4	4	2	5	4
Personal selling	4	4	4	4	2	2
Total	77	73	88	73	65	62

Table 2.1 — Competitive Analysis

Section 2.1.2 Opportunity Analysis

The second component of a communications analysis is the opportunity analysis. This section should be a byproduct or outcome of conducting the competitive analysis. Some questions which are helpful in the opportunity analysis are:

1. Are there customers that the competition is ignoring or not serving?
2. Which markets are heavily saturated and have intense competition?
3. Are the benefits of competing goods and services being clearly articulated to our customers?
4. Are there opportunities to build relationships with customers using a slightly different marketing approach than competitors are currently using?
5. Are there opportunities that are not being pursued, or is our brand positioned with a cluster of other companies in such a manner that it cannot stand out?

The opportunity analysis reveals various communication opportunities that can be exploited. These opportunities exist in four situations. The first is when there is an unfilled market niche. The second appears when the competition is doing a poor job of meeting the needs of customers. The third situation occurs when a company has a distinct competence to offer. The fourth is when a unique or superior method of communicating with potential customers exists. Other opportunities may result from market growth, lifestyle changes, resolving problems associated with current solutions, positive market perceptions about your business, or ability to offer greater value that will create a demand for your products.

Willamette Furniture has several potential opportunities. First was the opportunity to sell furniture through direct distribution channels that had not been tapped extensively by competitors. One reason for this opening was the rise in technology-savvy business executives and small business owners. Some hold an appreciation of and a desire for office furniture that is elegant but is also high-tech in its configuration and design. Willamette has an additional chance to market small business owners and home office businesspeople. This market has not previously been pursued, especially by larger firms.

To complete section 2.1.2, indicate time frames around opportunities whenever possible. Ask if the time frame is an ongoing opportunity or if rather it is a window of opportunity. How critical is timing? While the ideal is to pursue ongoing opportunities, sometimes firms have to take advantage of shorter windows of opportunities that are only open for a brief time.

2.1.2 Opportunity Analysis

An analysis of the high-end computer furniture market reveals several opportunities for Willamette Furniture. In reviewing these opportunities, consideration was given to company strengths and weaknesses as well as the competitive threats we face. The following are opportunities Willamette Furniture is ready to pursue:

- Opportunity for new channels of direct distribution, specifically sales through the Internet and catalogs targeted to each specific market.
- A specific niche of the office furniture market exists: consumers who appreciate quality materials (cherry and oak), ergonomics, and technology as well as the integration of those components. Consumers in this niche are more computer literate than the last generation and desire furniture that can hold computers.
- This new generation of corporate executives, small business owners, and home office users possesses a far greater appreciation of technology, along with an understanding of the needs which arise from implementing technology, such as the importance of a

> quality office environment which contains computers and other electronic tools in a usable and logical fashion.
>
> - The small business owner and the home office person have not been aggressively pursued by high-end office furniture manufacturers. The common belief is that these individuals make purchases from retail show rooms, dealers, and outlets such as Ethan Allen. The opportunity to focus direct marketing programs on these two segments has not been fully realized.

Section 2.1.3 Target Market Analysis

A target market analysis is a search for viable market segments. It begins with examination of the various potential customers that may buy your product. It is important to examine all feasible markets regardless of their size and attractiveness. Once this is accomplished then you can choose the most attractive markets.

The first step is to identify specific purchasing groups. Consumer groups make purchases based on common needs, attitudes, or interests. For a market segment to be considered a usable group for a specific marketing communications campaign, it should pass the following tests.

- The individuals or businesses in the market segment are similar in nature. Members will have the same needs, attitudes, interests, and opinions. This means persons or businesses within the segment are homogenous.
- The market segment differs from the population as a whole. Segments are distinct from other segments and the general population.
- The market segment is large enough to be financially viable to target with a separate marketing campaign.
- The market segment can be reached through some type of media or marketing communications method.

Once you have finished your market segmentation analysis, then a decision should be made on how each market will be segmented. This includes asking several questions, such as: How will we segment the consumer market? How will products reach the various distribution channels? How will we segment the business-to-business market?

Part of the segmentation decision includes not only selecting target markets that will be pursued; the other part is noting which groups will *not* be chosen. In most cases, the choices made regarding target markets determine the distribution channels to be utilized.

The second step is to describe the target markets in detail. Include demographic, psychographic, and behavioral information. The more information that is provided, the easier it is for the creatives to do their work. For instance, simply understanding that the target market consumers are males aged 25-40 is not sufficient. Adding information, such as that they like to fish and hunt, they prefer living in rural areas, and they hold conservative beliefs improves everyone's perception of the target market. More specific information can then be recorded. The table entitled Market Analysis serves this purpose for your IMC plan in section 2.1.3.

The next task in a target market analysis is estimating the size of market segment. A market is worthwhile when it is large enough to create profits. Your estimate should include the current size of the market and a projection of future growth trends. This information will then be placed in table entitled Target Market Forecast on your Plan Pro disk.

The Target Market Forecast table summarizes information about the market segments that have been chosen. The market analysis should focus on potential customers rather than actual customers. For example, Willamette Furniture estimated there are 36 million home offices in the United States. Still, they believe that only 27% of these home offices, or 4.4 million, represent a potential market for furniture. Further, Willamette estimates that only 20% of the 4.4 million would be a viable market for high-end office furniture. Thus, for this target market, Willamette would estimate that the number of potential customers is 880,000.

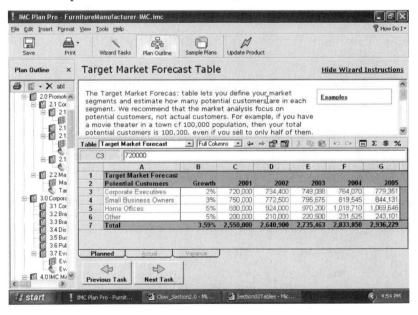

Figure 2.3 — By completing the Target Market Forecast table in the IMC Plan Pro software, the graphs in this section will be automatically produced.

After completing an estimate of the size of each market, suggest a five year trend for the market. The growth rate column in the table on your disk uses a straight-line growth rate model that applies to the first year and then is used to calculate the estimated growth for future years. You can also override these calculations by simply typing in the market numbers you want to show for future years, regardless of growth rates.

2.1.3 Target Market Analysis

A person in our target market is someone seeking fine furniture that also accommodates the latest in technology. The individual appreciates old fashioned fine woods and fine woodworking. This person can be located in a company's corporate towers, in a small or medium business, or in a home office. The common bond is the appreciation of quality and the lack of price constraints.

Our marketing campaign focuses on four target segments:

- **Corporate Executives:** The Bureau of Labor Statistics (http://stats.bls.gov) reports that there are 14.4 million executive, administrative, and managerial employees in the United States. The number is growing at a rate of 1.6% per year. We estimate the top 5% of that number, 720,000, is our market. This number should also grow at the same 1.6% annual rate.
- **Small Business Owners and Executives:** According to the most recent data available from the Small Business Administration (SBA), there are between 13 and 16 million small businesses (500 employees or fewer) in the United States. This includes about 5.5 million employers and 11 million self-employed people. The top 5% of these 15 million individuals constitute our potential market of 750,000 customers. We estimate growth at 2.5%, a composite of different sources.
- **Home Offices:** According to a story in Home Office Computing magazine, there are 36 million home offices in the United States. This means there is a home office in

about 27% of the households in the U.S. The U.S. census reports that in 1997 there were 16 million households in this country with incomes of more than $100,000 per year. The 27% of those that have home offices are our potential market. In other words, 4.4 million households (of 132 million total). Our market is the top 20% of those, or 880,000 consumers, which we estimate is growing at 5% per year.

- **Other:** We will also sell to some buyers outside the United States and outside of these targeted market segments. We estimate 200,000 additional potential customers, a number that should grow at a rate of 5% per year.

Consumers in these target markets want more than just office furniture. They need personal computing technology combined with office furniture. Therefore, keyboards and monitors must be at the correct height, there must be proper channels for cables, and they want other amenities. Our target customer prefers all of these features in an attractive piece of furniture. These individuals are looking for quality wood products with superior craftsmanship in the item. In other words, we cannot merely sell office furniture. Willamette sells design, workmanship, fine materials, and a total-quality office environment.

Target Market Forecast Potential	Growth	2001	2002	2003	2004	2005	CAGR
Corporate Executives	2%	720,000	734,400	749,088	764,070	779,351	2.00%
Small Business Owners	3%	750,000	772,500	795,675	819,545	844,131	3.00%
Home Offices	5%	880,000	924,000	970,200	1,018,710	1,069,646	5.00%
Other	5%	200,000	210,000	220,500	231,525	243,101	5.00%
Total	3.59%	2,550,000	2,640,900	2,735,463	2,833,850	2,936,229	3.59%

Table 2.2 — Target Market Forecast

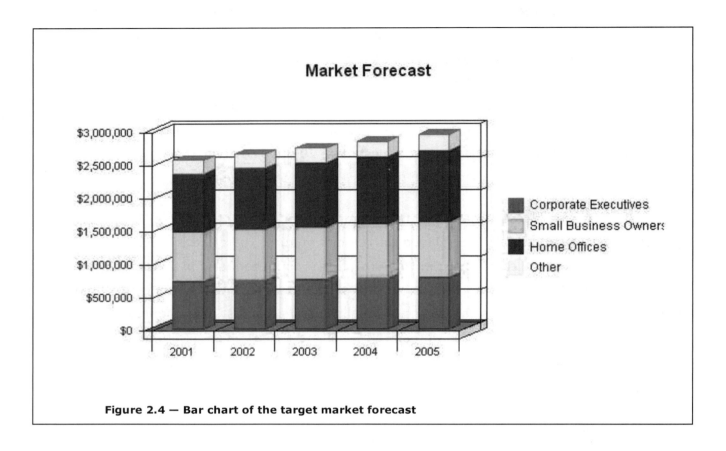

Figure 2.4 — Bar chart of the target market forecast

Section 2.1.4 Customer Analysis

The fourth part of a communications analysis is a customer analysis. It is crucial to understand your customers. While it is true that specific demographic information is valuable, it takes more than demographics to prepare effective communications. In this section, each target market is described in terms of demographics, psychographics, and behaviors. Psychographic information helps the marketing team understand each target segment's attitudes, interests, and opinions. For example, describing a target segment as one that enjoys sports and outdoors activities and has an interest in preserving the environment is a much richer than just saying the target segment consists of females, ages 20-35, with incomes from $30,000 to $60,000.

Another aspect of a customer analysis is finding out why customers buy particular products. What benefits do they seek? What attributes are important? What personal values, needs, or wants does the product provide for the customer? In the Willamette Furniture example given below, the primary issues that are relevant to a purchase decision are discussed for each group. This information is invaluable when preparing the advertisements and other marketing communication pieces.

2.1.4 Customer Analysis

Willamette Furniture focuses on a special kind of customer: the kind of person who enjoys high-quality office furniture that can be customized to display modern technology, including personal computers, scanners, Internet connections, and other high-tech items. This customer might be employed by a large corporation, a small or medium business, or work in a personal home office with or without a home-office business. What is important to the customer is elegance, fine workmanship, ease of use, ergonomics, and practicality.

Willamette does not intend to try to satisfy every user of office furniture. Instead, only those who are most demanding constitute our customers. The objective is to address the needs of high-end buyers who are willing to pay more for quality.

In our markets, potential customers appreciate two attributes: the quality of furniture workmanship and the excellence of the design. These individual understand that the match of technology and ergonomics that Willamette is in the unique position to offer. Three groups are important:

- **Corporate Executives:** Our corporate executive customers are typically between 40 and 65 years of age. They earn annual salaries in excess of $200,000. While these executives are not heavy computer users, the primary issue when selecting office furniture is prestige. The decision in selecting furniture for the executive office, however, is normally left to the office staff.
- **Small Business Owners and Executives:** A small business owner tends to be slightly younger, 30 to 65 with a salary of $50,000 or higher. In most cases, the business is an entrepreneurial venture started by the individual himself or herself. The primary issue in selecting furniture is comfort. This means the small business person is normally involved in the purchase decision. A small business customer routinely uses computers and is familiar with other technical equipment.

- **Home Offices:** The home office market segment consists of individuals between the ages of 25 and 65. These customers typically earn incomes in excess of $100,000. Space is a major consideration for these individuals, because many work out of their homes. Many of the businesses are computer-related. Consequently, the individual is a high user of modern technology. Configuration of equipment is important. Often the customer runs a one-person-business operation. Therefore, workmanship, ease of use, and ergonomics are key issues in the selection process. Even for home offices that are not business related, space and configuration are primary features.

An important attractive feature of these markets is the potential future growth rate. Home offices and the international market should experience at least a 5% rate of annual growth. The small business owner market is anticipated to grow at a 2.5% annual rate while the corporate executive market's annual growth rate is expected to be around 1.6%. The growth in these target markets should allow for steady growth over the next five years for Willamette Furniture.

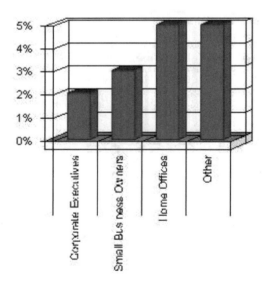

Figure 2.5 — Bar chart of the Target Market 5-Year Growth Rate

Section 2.2 Market Segmentation Analysis

Market segmentation efforts are the second component of the promotions opportunity analysis (all of Section 2.0 on your disk). To complete the market segmentation section of the IMC plan, you will need to find ways to build brand loyalty and improve the odds of success for a marketing plan. Market segments are found in three general areas: (1) consumer markets, (2) distribution channels, and (3) business-to-business markets. Consider each source as you write your plan.

Consumer Segmentation

In many instances, end-users or consumers are the primary target market for a firm's offerings. An effective market segmentation analysis suggests sets of consumers who are potential buyers. These buyers have things in common, such as common attitudes, interests, or needs. Typical methods of segmenting the consumer market include the following:

- Demographic
- Psychographics
- Generations
- Geographic
- Geodemographics
- Benefits
- Usage

Demographics are population characteristics. Some of the most common demographic categories that are used for the purposes of segmentation include gender, age, income, race, educational level, and ethnicity. For instance, messages are targeted to women, seniors, high and low wage earners, college graduates, and various minorities on a daily basis.

Psychographics are patterns of behavior that reveal a person's attitudes, interests, and opinions (AIO). One group of consumers sees themselves as "high rollers," or people with an acquired taste for things associated with affluence. Another group may be identified as "geeks," or people with a natural affinity for computer technology. These groups are more likely to be influenced by messages tuned to their tastes.

Generational segmentation occurs when marketing messages are targeted at generational cohorts. Some of the most notable groups include baby boomers, generation X, and generation Y. Messages aimed at older cohorts, such as the "greatest generation" World War II cohort are beginning to decline. Generational cohorts share common memories, emotional experiences, and even feelings about songs and movies. These can be reached through emotional advertisements that help cohort members recall these moments in positive ways.

Geographic information can be used to locate consumers in a geographic area or region. There are times when all of the people in a geographic area are potential customers. For example, *Sports Illustrated* creates "championship editions" of the magazine targeted primarily at customers who live near a championship-winning college or professional sports team.

Geodemographic segmentation is a hybrid form in which the marketing team adds geographic data to psychographic information. Some neighborhoods, for example, are largely populated by people sharing common values and interests. These clusters of consumers can be targeted with direct mail and Internet based messages.

Benefit segmentation focuses on the qualities of the product. A milk commercial spelling out the benefits of the product for growing children is one example of this approach. Note that the same approach can be combined with other demographic information, leading to an ad featuring the role milk can play in slowing osteoporosis for older women.

Usage segmentation is designed to market goods to heavy users of a product or service. Video games tend to be targeted to adolescent and teenage boys, because they are the heavy users. Wine clubs look for ways to send messages to people who regularly consume wine, as opposed to casual or social drinkers.

State the consumer target markets your company intends to pursue in your IMC plan. This helps the company focus all other marketing efforts more precisely.

Channels Segmentation

Segmentation can also be performed within the channel of distribution. To do so, you can examine how your product moves from your production to the end-user. This procedure varies for every product and for the type of business. Some producers utilize wholesalers or distributors to move products from production to retail outlets. Others sell directly to retail outlets. Others use direct marketing and sell straight to the consumer. Direct marketing can be based on catalogs, telemarketing, and the Internet.

The goal of channel segmentation analysis is to decide which distribution channels best meet the company's marketing objectives. In many cases, channel segmentation results in using more than one distribution approach. For example, Willamette discovered an opportunity to sell through the Internet and catalogs, because it is an under-utilized distribution channel in the industry. Rather than relying solely on the typical distribution channel of wholesalers and retailers to sell their furniture, Willamette's executives believed that selling through direct channels provides a better approach.

Business-to-Business Segmentation

The final approach to segmentation features business-to-business markets. There are differences between marketing to businesses and marketing to individual customers. Still, many of the segmentation methods used are similar. For example, two common objectives of both forms of segmentation are: (1) to provide better customer service and (2) to group homogeneous customers into clusters in order to enhance the marketing program. Business-to-business market segments include those identified by the:

- NAICS/SIC code
- Type of business
- Size of business
- Geographic location
- Product's usage
- Purchase decision process
- Customer's value

The *NAICS/SIC code* approach is oriented at finding the specific industry to be targeted. NAICS stands for "North American Industry Classification System." The code note specific market groups, such as physicians, chiropractors, optometrists, and dentists as groups that are part of the Ambulatory Health Care Providers category. Most marketers now use the NAICS code rather than the SIC (Standard Industry Code) to identify market segments.

The *type of business* approach is similar to the NAICS code method. One difference is that other features are introduced to categorize the market. Some examples of these differences include "low-cost/high volume" customers as opposed to "high end" businesses.

Figure 2.6 — This pie chart highlights the business market segments for Willamette Furniture and was produced by the IMC Plan Pro software from the data provided in the Market Segmentation Analysis table.

Company size is another segmentation component. Smaller companies have different needs than larger firms. Marketing efforts aimed at small companies may highlight personal service and forms of help such as inventory control and credit. Messages geared to larger firms often focus on price, delivery, or other features.

Geographic location may be used to discover some business-to-business market segments. Silicon Valley is a location utilized by many computer companies. In the Midwest, agricultural products can be targeted at corporate farming companies.

Product usage is another means used to find business market segments, since a product or service may have a variety of uses. Financial, transportation, and shipping services carry a variety of options that may be sold to individual companies. In the hotel industry, conferences and trade shows are primary sources of revenue in some locations. These hotels market services to other businesses or groups that hold such conventions.

Segmentation by purchase decision process is geared to customers who arrive at a purchase choice in different ways. Three groups to think about when using this method are: (1) first-time prospects, (2) novices, and (3) sophisticates. First-time prospects are companies that have never purchased a particular product or service but have started evaluating vendors. Novices are first-time customers who have made a recent purchase of the product or service. Sophisticates are companies that have already purchased the product and are ready to rebuy or have just made repeat purchases.

Each interacts with vendors in different ways based on special needs and the levels of information already held by buyers.

Customer value segmentation involves describing which customers offer the best potential revenues and profits. Some accounts are labor intensive and do not yield much income. Others may require a great deal of work but have high payoffs. Others still are those that don't consume many marketing resources but do contribute to cash flow and profit. Each group is assigned a value. Then, messages and marketing efforts can then be modified to fit the individual segment.

In section 2.2 of your IMC plan, all market segments should be identified. There are many advantages to conducting a thorough market segmentation analysis. These advantages include:

1. Helping marketers identify company strengths and weaknesses as well as opportunities in the marketplace.
2. Working toward the goal of matching what the firm does best with the most enticing sets of customers.
3. Clarifying marketing objectives associated with individual target markets.
4. More precisely focusing budgeting expenditures or consumer groups and business segments.
5. Linking company strategies and tactics to select groups of customers.

Therefore, as you complete this section of your IMPC plan, remember that this information is a primary guide for all of the activities that follow. Here is the end-result of Willamette's segmentation analysis.

2.2 Segmentation Analysis

Willamette's primary segmentation analysis reveals target markets in three areas: (1) business-to-business, which is the largest segment; (2) end-user consumers, and (3) the direct market distribution channel.

Business-to-business customers can be identified by noting size and type of business. Those companies seeking high quality furnishings that are willing to pay a higher price are the primary group.

Within the **consumer market**, which is the home office target segment, the market will be segmented by the personal income. The rationale for this segmentation approach is that Willamette knows it cannot satisfy every user of office furniture. The goal of this segmentation approach is to address the needs of the high-end buyer, who is willing to pay more for quality.

Direct marketing distribution channels provide a unique opportunity. They represent the opportunity to sell our products using the Internet and catalogs send by direct mail. These venues are not used by the competition to any degree, which makes them a clear opportunity for Willamette.

The table below provides a description of each market segment based on our segmentation approach.

Market Segments	Computer Usage	Age	Income	Issues	Decision Maker
Corporate Executives	Medium	40-65	$200,000 and up	Prestige	Staff
Small Business Owners	Medium	30-65	$50,000 and up	Comfort	User
Home Offices	High	25-65	$100,000 and up	Space	User
Other	-	-	-	-	-

Table 2.3 — Market Segmentation Analysis

The pie chart below provides a graphical representation of the approximate size of each of our market segments. Our largest market segment is the home office segment, estimated to be 880,000. The small business owner is our second largest market segment estimated at 750,000. We estimate the size of the corporate executive segment to approximately 720,000.

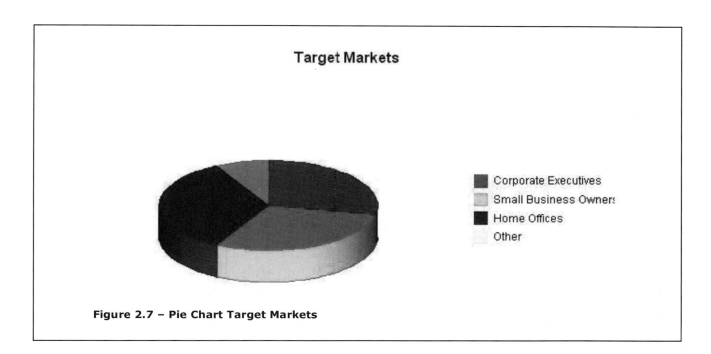

Figure 2.7 – Pie Chart Target Markets

Section 3
Corporate Strategies

Corporate strategies form a major portion of the foundation for an effective marketing program. Corporate strategies drive all company activities. This section of the IMC plan is where you address how these strategies affect the product or service being sold. Remember that in some cases the product for which you are developing an IMC plan is just one of many products offered by the company.

Section 3.0

Section 3.0 begins with a summary paragraph highlighting the key points of the overall corporate strategy. Corporate strategies should guide you to the key marketing strategies that you intend to implement. Details for each marketing strategy are spelled out in the sub-sections that follow. It is important to make sure that what is spelled out in sections 3.1 through 3.6 matches with the summary you provide in section 3.0. You may need to go back and revise your opening statement after you completed the details in all of the other sections related to corporate strategies.

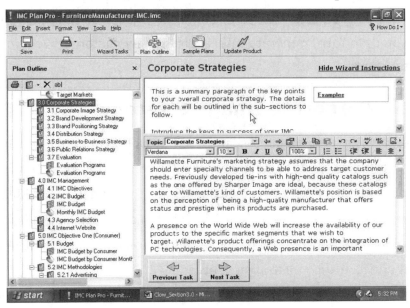

Figure 3.1 — Section 3.0 of the IMC Plan addresses various corporate strategies.

3.0 Corporate Strategies

Willamette's image is based on perceptions that the company is a high-quality furniture manufacturer. Willamette's products offer status and prestige to discerning customers. The term that best describes our furniture is "elegance."

To build on and maintain this image, Willamette must move forward by developing new products aimed at the same target market. Efforts must also be made to attract customers in all potential markets and market segments. This includes a new emphasis on direct marketing.

To support our corporate strategy, all of our marketing efforts will be strategically integrated into the plan. This includes advertising, sales promotions, and trade promotions that are designed to maximize our communications efforts. The goal is to make sure each customer contact with Willamette Furniture reinforces what is already being said about the company. This should, in turn, generate interest from new customers looking for elegant high-end office furniture.

Section 3.1   Corporate Image Strategy

Effective IMC programs are built on the base provided by a clearly defined and understood corporate image. A corporate image summarizes what the company stands for as well as how the company is positioned in the market place. Whether it is the "good hands" of Allstate Insurance or the "good neighbors" at State Farm Insurance, the goal of image management is to create and maintain a stable impression in the minds of clients and customers. Fine-tuning and communicating the proper image is critical to an organization's success.

The first thing to keep in mind is that what organizational officials believe about the company is less important than what *consumers* believe about the company. Corporate names such as IBM, e-Bay, General Motors, Nike, and Exxon conjure various images in the minds of consumers, some positive and some less positive. The specific image of a firm may vary from person to person or business to business. Your goal should be to understand the overall or most general image of a firm, which is determined by the combined views of all publics. This image strongly influences customers as they make purchase decisions.

As you prepare section 3.1, your first task is to get a clear idea about the nature of the firm's current image. To do so, make sure all constituencies are included. Contact the company's customers, suppliers, and employees. This will help you to correctly discern the true nature of the image. You should also interview other consumers, especially non-customers. Once those in the firm understand how the company is currently being viewed, they are ready to make decisions about the image they wish to try to project in the future. Keep in mind four things that apply to managing a corporate image:

1. The image being projected must be an accurate portrayal of the firm and coincide with the goods and services being sold.
2. Reinforcing or rejuvenating a current image that is consistent with the view of consumers is easier to accomplish than changing an image which is well-established.
3. It is very difficult to change the images people hold regarding a given company. In some cases, modifying or developing a new image simply cannot be done
4. Any negative or bad press can quickly destroy an image that took years to build. Re-establishing or rebuilding the firm's image takes a great deal of time, once the damage to a firm's reputation has been done

Section 3.1 is the place where you summarize what the company stands for and what you want customers to believe about the company. Notice that Willamette Furniture Company's corporate image strategy is to be the preferred choice for high-end executive office furniture. If Willamette could describe its image using one word, that word would be "elegance."

3.1 Corporate Image Strategy

Willamette Furniture's corporate goal is to be the preferred choice for high-end executive office furniture. In addition to incorporating the various computer components within the furniture itself, Willamette furniture is ergonomically designed to provide maximum comfort and style.

Elegance is evident in every piece of Willamette furniture. Our attractive office furniture is designed for corporate executives, small business executives, and home offices. Our corporate image strategy is to make sure that existing and future customers to consider Willamette not just an option, but the best office furniture option, based on the company's longstanding reputation for quality and superior design.

Section 3.2   Brand Development Strategy

Many of the characteristics and benefits of a quality corporate image apply to brands as well. The primary difference between perceptions of an overall image versus a single brand is scope. Brands are assigned to a product or a group of complementary products. A corporate image includes every aspect of the company. The Procter and Gamble corporation carries many brands, including Tide, Cheer, and Bold laundry detergents, Crest and Gleem toothpastes, and Old Spice, Secret, and Sure deodorants.

There are many benefits to a strong and effective brand name. First, a powerful brand allows a company to charge more for its products. This increases gross margins on sales of each unit. A strong brand provides customers with assurances of quality. Consumers will then reduce the amount of search time allocated to the purchasing process. They will also consider fewer purchase alternatives, and mostly look at only those that offer a viable alternative to a known and preferred brand.

In mature markets, few tangible distinctions exist between competing products. When a substantial product improvement appears, it is usually quickly copied by competitors. Thus, only minor differences exist in many product categories. Even minor variations are hard to find. More than once, marketing research has been used to demonstrate that when brand names and labels are removed, consumers often find it difficult to distinguish between products and services (Pledge versus Endust, many beers and soft drinks, life insurance policies sold by different companies, flights on various airlines etc.). Therefore, it is vitally important to establish a strong brand name, one that stands out in the marketplace.

Your company has a strong brand when it passes several tests. First, typical consumers must be aware of the name. Second, the product is always considered among feasible brands to purchase. Third, consumers regard the brand as a good value. Fourth, they buy or use the product on a regular basis. A strong brand is one the consumers recommend to their family and friends.

Developing a strong brand begins with discovering why consumers buy a brand and why they re-buy the brand. Some good questions to ask include:

- What are the most compelling benefits of the product?
- What emotions are elicited by the brand either during or after the purchase?
- What is the one word that best describes the brand?
- What is important to consumers in the purchase of the product?

Once the answers to these questions are known, a company is ready to go forward with the brand development part of the marketing campaign.

Two things can help a company create stronger brand. First, the name must be repeatedly promoted in advertisements. Repetition helps to capture an individual's attention. Repetition also increases the odds that a message will be stored in a customer's knowledge structures.

Second, the brand name must be associated with its most prominent characteristic. For example, many consumers associate Crest with "cavity prevention." Coca-Cola seeks to associate its name with a product that is "refreshing." For Volvo, the impression is "safety." For BMW, it is "performance driving."

The goal of brand development is to set a product apart from its competitors. Marketing experts seek to identify the "one thing" that a brand can stand for, that consumers will recognize, and that is salient to consumers. When these tasks are successfully completed, more powerful brand recognition and brand loyalty are possible.

Another aspect of brand development is designing or revising the corporate or brand logo. Quality logos should accomplish four things. First, they should be easily recognizable. Second, they should be familiar. Third, they should elicit a consensual meaning among those in the firm's target market. Fourth, and finally, a quality logo evokes positive feelings about the product.

Logos can be another valuable tool in an IMC plan. Pictures and other visual images are processed by the mind faster than words. As a result, logos can be easily recognized by consumers. In a marketing program, logo recognition should occur at two levels. First, individuals should remember seeing the logo in the past. The image should be stored in such a way that when it is seen at a retail store or in an advertisement, the consumer's memory is jogged. Second, the logo reminds consumers of the brand or corporate name. This reminder should elicit positive feelings regarding the brand name and conjure up that one idea or quality associated with the brand.

Successful logos elicit what are known as "shared meanings" across consumers. When a logo results in a consensual meaning among customers, the outcome is known as "stimulus codability." Logos with high stimulus codability have a common meaning within a culture or subculture (such as the Prudential Rock or the Mercedes emblem). Logos with a high degree of codability are more easily recognized and can be linked more easily to a product or service. On the other hand, when a logo has a low degree of codability, the company must spend more money on advertising. Recognition of the logo is gained through familiarity rather than the stimulus codability. For example, Nike spent a considerable amount of resources making their Swoosh recognizable to those in various target markets, since the Swoosh by itself did not conjure any specific image of the firm early in its life.

In your analysis of the brand development strategy and in the selection of a logo, questions that may be helpful to address include:

- How was the name of your brand chosen?
- What does it symbolize when people hear the name?
- How will the brand name be incorporated into a memorable logo?
- Will the brand name be included or will you try to build the brand around a logo alone?
- How will you make the brand relevant to consumers?

Figure 3.2 — In the Brand Development section of the IMC is a description of the brand name and logo.

Many brands are more than just names. A quality brand communicates the attributes, benefits, values, and even the "personality" of a product or service. When Kentucky Fried Chicken changed its name to KFC, the goal was to create a more "modern" feel to the company.

The Willamette Furniture uses the corporation's name as its brand name. Instead of using Willamette as an example of brand development, you can view the section of your IMC Plan Pro disk featuring the Boulder Stop. The company is another of the IMC sample plans provided on your disk. The Boulder Stop is a retail store selling snow skiing equipment combined with a café where skiers can relax and enjoy a warm beverage. Here is the brand development strategy section.

3.2 Brand Development Strategy

The brand name of "The Boulder Stop" was selected because of its symbolic reference to stopping at the Boulder, Smith Rock. The brand name is readily identified with rock climbing and incorporated into our logo, as shown. Further, the name suggests a company offering rock climbing supplies but also one that offers climbers a place to stop, have coffee, and discuss rock climbing experiences.

The name "The Boulder Stop" has a high level of stimulus codability. Consensual meanings should be possible across the various segments of rock climbers as well as non-rock climbing enthusiasts. In developing advertisements and other promotions, the brand name can be incorporated directly into the message, which will aid in message recall and message comprehension.

The Boulder Stop logo incorporates the name with the symbol of a large rock. Consistent with the brand image strategy, the brand development strategy and the brand positioning strategy, The Boulder Stop will use the tagline "Only One Stop! The Boulder Stop!" This tagline conveys the concept that the Boulder Stop is the source for everything a climber needs. It also conveys the concept of quality in that the customer does not need to shop at any other store. Further, offering coffee and a lodge-type atmosphere allows climbers to meet some of their social needs in the same place, The Boulder Stop.

Section 3.3   Brand Positioning Strategy

A third ingredient in effective corporate and brand image management is dealing with brand positioning. Positioning is creating a perception regarding the nature of a company and its products relative to the competition in the consumer's mind. Position is created by variables such as the quality of products, prices charged, methods of distribution, image, and other factors.

Brand positioning consists of two elements. First, the position is established relative to the competition. Second, a product's position exists in the minds of consumers. Although firms may attempt to position products through advertising and other marketing communications programs, consumers ultimately determine the positions of a firm's products. To be effective, the marketing team must either reinforce what consumers already believe about a product and its brand name or shift the consumer's view towards a more desirable position. The former strategy is certainly easier to accomplish than the latter. The goal of positioning is to find that niche in a consumer's mind that a product can occupy.

Positioning is clearly evident in companies such as Proctor and Gamble, VF Corporation, Sara Lee Corporation, and Campbell Soups. These firms also use positioning to help prevent cannibalism among various brands within a product category. For example, Campbell produces five different types of V8 juice. For individuals who are concerned about calories and fat content, Campbell offers a V8 with no fat and only 50 calories. Campbell offers a low Sodium version of V8 for individuals on a low-sodium diet, a spicy hot version for individuals who want something with more taste or who need a mixer, and a calcium enriched version for individuals wanting more calcium, potassium or vitamins A and C.

Effective positioning can be achieved in seven different ways. Although companies may try to use two or three approaches, normally such efforts result in confusion on the part of the consumer. As a result, the best method is to use one of these approaches consistently:

- Attribute
- Competitors
- Use or application
- Price/quality relationship
- Product user
- Product class
- Cultural symbol

An *attribute* is a product trait or characteristic which sets it apart from other products. A few years ago, an attempt was made to show Budweiser as having the advantage of "freshness." The company even added a "born on" date to the label, seeking to make this distinction in the consumer's mind.

Using *competitors* to garner a position in the consumer's mind is another common tactic. The idea is to take one brand and contrast it with the position of another. For example, for several years Avis relied on a series of advertisements comparing itself to Hertz. In the ads, Avis admitted the company was not number one. Instead, the advertisement went on to explain the advantage that second place brought to consumers. Second-place Avis was willing to "try harder" for business.

Use or application positioning is based on the creation of a memorable set of uses for a product. This approach has long been utilized by Arm and Hammer. Consumers know that the baking soda can also be used in a refrigerator as a deodorizer. Arm and Hammer has also been featured as a co-brand in toothpaste, creating yet another use for the product.

The *price/quality relationship* form of positioning is often used by businesses on the extremes of the price range. At the top end, businesses emphasize high quality while at the bottom end, low prices are emphasized. Hallmark cards cost more, but are for those who "only want to send the very best." Other firms seek to be a "low price leader," with no corresponding statement about quality. Wal-Mart stresses everyday low prices.

A *product user positioning strategy* distinguishes a brand or product by clearly specifying who might use it. Apple Computers originally positioned themselves as the computer for educational institutions. Although this strategy helped them grow rapidly, Apple had a difficult time convincing businesses that their computers could be used in the business arena. Apple had done such a good job with their original positioning strategy that it became difficult to change people's view of the company until the iPod products were introduced.

Some firms position the brand or company within a particular *product class.* Orange juice was long considered to be part of the breakfast drink product class. Years ago, those in the industry decided to create advertisements which were designed to move orange juice into a new product class, with slogans such as "it's not just for breakfast anymore." This re-positioning became successful and many consumers now consider orange juice at anytime during the day. The move was successful because orange juice can be seen as a "healthy" choice. On the other hand, if the product class is viewed as beverages, then orange juice would have been competing with giants such as Pepsi and Coke, and would have been much less likely to succeed. Identifying a product with a *cultural symbol* is difficult. When the approach is successful it becomes a strong competitive advantage for a firm. One well-known example of this type of type positioning strategy was achieved by Chevrolet. During the summer, GM advertises Chevrolet as being as American as baseball and apple pie. Stetson identifies its cologne with an American cowboy and the spirit of the west.

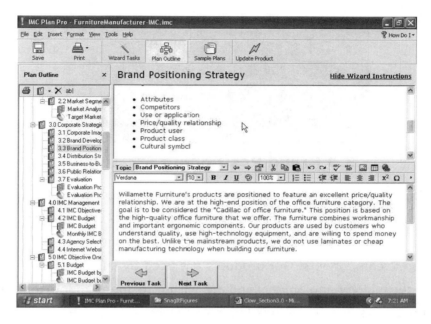

Figure 3.3 — The IMC Plan Pro software provides a list of the various positioning strategies as part of the instructions for this section of your IMC Plan.

Brand positioning can be applied to business-to-business marketing efforts. Crowne Plaza, a sub-brand of Holiday Inn, has developed a positioning strategy for upscale business travelers based on attributes. The company provides services and amenities that business travelers desire. At the same time, the company does not provide amenities that might be considered extravagant, so that rooms can be charged to expense accounts.

As you develop a positioning strategy, remember the positioning difference should be relevant to consumers. This difference or benefit should be considered useful in the buying decision-making process. Brand positioning is a critical part of image and brand name management. Consumers have an extensive set of purchasing options. They are able to seek out products with specific advantages or attributes. Effective positioning, by whatever tactic chosen, can increase sales and strengthen the long-term sales of individual products and those of total organization. As you write the positioning statement, the following questions that might help:

- What is your target market's most important market need?
- How does your product meet that need?
- Who is the main competition?
- How is your product better than that of the competition?
- How do your customers perceive your brand in relation to the competition?

The Willamette Furniture company's brand positioning strategy for the entire line is shown next. As you can see, there is a strong tie-in with statements about the company's image.

3.3 Brand Positioning Strategy

Willamette Furniture's products are positioned based on an excellent price/quality relationship. We are at the high-end position of the office furniture category. The goal is to be considered the best quality office furniture. The furniture combines workmanship and important ergonomic components. Our products are used by customers who understand quality, use high-technology equipment, and are willing to spend money on the best. Unlike the mainstream products, we do not use laminates or cheap manufacturing technology when building our furniture. There are many computer furniture manufacturers and there are also many computer lovers. Few furniture companies target computer lovers who want elegant furniture. Even putting together unassembled furniture is a positive experience for our customers. Our assembly strategy is based on interlocking wood pieces of such high quality that assembly is simple and pleasant. Assembly actually becomes a feature that enhances the sense of quality associated with the furniture.

Section 3.4   Distribution Strategy

A distribution strategy describes the physical movement of products from the producer to individual or organizational consumers. Distribution includes the transfer of ownership and risk, transportation, and warehousing. It also involves choosing the appropriate channels of distribution. Typical members of the distribution channel include wholesalers, distributors, agents, and retailers. A well-designed distribution strategy means the delivery of products to the end consumer is both efficient and effective.

When constructing a distribution strategy, the first decision is whether to use direct or indirect channels. A direct channel has no intermediaries. Instead, the manufacturer sells directly to the final consumer. As you have seen, Willamette sells some of its furniture directly to small business owners using the Internet.

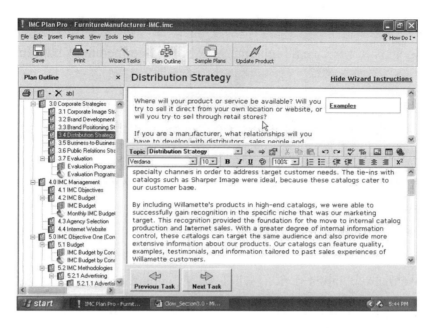

Figure 3.4 — In this section, Willamette describes the distribution strategy that will be used by their company.

An indirect channel of distribution involves one or more intermediaries between the manufacturer and the consumer. When a bakery sells its chocolate chip cookies to the Fresh Market in North Carolina or to the Amish Market in New York City, an indirect channel of distribution is being used. A bakery may also utilize a distributor, such as Bay View Distributing, to market their cookies to retail outlets. This adds an additional layer to the channel of distribution.

The second decision to be made is the type of distribution. Three strategies are possible: (1) intensive, (2) selective, or (3) exclusive distribution. Each of the three choices matches different types of products and companies.

An intensive distribution strategy is designed to achieve full market coverage by making the product accessible to all target consumers when and wherever they want it. The idea is to place the product in every available location or outlet, even when a location is not profitable by itself. Many convenience goods, such as chewing gum, chips, and soft drinks, are intensively distributed.

A selective distribution strategy means limiting distribution to a select group of retailers in each area. The objective is to obtain reasonable sales volume and profits in each location that is selected. Unprofitable outlets are dropped or are not selected in the first place. This approach allows the company to keep control over the marketing program. Selective distribution is used for a wide variety of consumer shopping goods.

When a company uses an exclusive distribution strategy, the product is sold by only one or two retail outlets per geographic area. This type of distribution is intended to create prestige for the company's products. The manufacturer must provide strong support and service to retail outlets that are used. The goal is to exercise a high control over the intermediaries handling the company's products.

In developing your distribution strategy, some important questions to ask include:
- Will you use a direct channel of distribution, an indirect channel, or both?
- Where will your good or service be available?
- Will you try to sell it direct from your own location or website, or will you try to sell through retail stores?
- If you are selling through retail outlets, which outlets?
- Will you use an intensive, selective, or exclusive distribution strategy?
- Will you use intermediaries such as wholesalers, agents, brokers, or distributors? If so, which ones?

As you can see in the following example, Willamette Furniture uses an exclusive approach in the retail marketplace combined with direct marketing efforts. This approach best matches the products, image, and quality level of the company.

3.4 Distribution Strategy

There are two channels of distribution for Willamette furniture, (1) using intermediaries and (2) direct marketing.

The first component in our program is an exclusive distribution strategy. In the high-end furniture market, particularly in our niche, product features are extremely important. Our target customer does not make a selection based on price. The ergonomics, design, accommodation of the computer features within the high-quality feel of good wood, are much more important. In each geographic area, one or two retail outlets will be chosen. We will work closely with these retailers to make sure that the purchasing experience is as elegant as our furniture. Our goal is to win the best quality display space in the retail store.

Some high-end retailers, such as the Sharper Image, offer tie-ins with catalogs. These tie-ins are ideal, because these catalogs cater to our customer base. By including

Willamette's products in high-end catalogs, we are able to successfully maintain recognition in the specific niche that was our marketing target.

The recognition of the Willamette brand provides the foundation for the move to our own internal catalog production and Internet sales, which is the basis of our other channel, direct distribution. Many purchases of office furniture are made through direct contacts with manufacturers. In direct sales these customers, price and quality are critical. Direct buyers want to make trouble-free purchases at a great price. This makes reliable delivery and easy assembly as important as product quality.

Marketing research indicates that 51% of the total sales volume in the office furniture market goes through the retail channel. Most of these sales are made by major national chains. Another 23% goes through the direct sales channel, although in this case direct sales include sales by distributors who offer items from multiple manufacturers. Most of the remainder, 18%, is sold directly to buyers by catalogs, by personal selling, or through the Internet.

Section 3.5   Business-to-Business Strategy

Many types of goods and services are sold from one business to another. Goods include major equipment such as bulldozers and mainframe computers, accessories such as calculators and coffee makers, fabricated and component parts such as spark plugs for automobiles, process materials such as cement and plastic, as well as maintenance, repair, and operating supplies. Services that are sold to businesses include health insurance, telephone service, janitorial services, legal services, and consulting services. It is possible your IMC plan will require a business-to-business strategy.

To develop this portion of this plan, you first must understand how most business purchase decisions are made. While people make business purchasing decisions, some things are different. First, most of the time, several individuals must work together to reach a final choice. Further, corporate policies create guidelines that vendors must follow. And, buyers often follow decision rules as purchase decisions are made. Factors such as budgets, costs, and profit considerations are likely to influence the final purchase choice. Two key ingredients of business-to-business marketing strategies are finding out who belongs to the buying center and understanding the various types of purchases.

The Buying Center

A business purchase is seldom made by a single individual. Since several people are involved, the purchasing process becomes much more complex. The individuals involved in the business buying decision are called members of the buying center. The following roles are played by members of the buying:

- Users
- Buyers
- Influencers
- Deciders
- Gatekeepers

Users are the people who will actually use the product or service after it has been purchased. When the product is office supplies, users are likely to the secretarial staff. A service, such as a corporate credit card, is used by members of the sales staff.

Buyers are the individuals given the formal responsibility of making the final purchase. In larger organizations, buyers are either purchasing agents or members of the purchasing department. In smaller organizations, the buyer may be the owner or president of the company, a manager, or even a secretary.

Influencers are people who shape purchasing decisions by providing the information or criteria utilized in evaluating alternatives. Influencers are often formally appointed as part of a committee charged with selecting a vendor. In other firms the process is less formal. For example, an engineer may describe the specifications for a particular product that his or her department needs.

Deciders are the individuals who authorize decisions. They are often purchasing agents. In large organizations, purchase decisions may be finalized by a financial officer, a vice-president, or even by the president of the company. Whoever agrees to cut loose funds to complete a purchase is the decider.

The *gatekeeper* controls the flow of information to members of the buying center. Gatekeepers keep people informed about potential alternatives and decision rules that are being used. The gatekeeper also lets members know when certain alternatives have been rejected. In some situations, it is not a specific individual who is the gatekeeper, but rather a gatekeeping function in which members notify each other regarding various events associated with the purchase.

These five roles often overlap. A gatekeeper may also be the buyer. The purchasing department normally determines what information is given to members of the buying center, and they usually control the amount of access a salesperson has to members of the buying center. Also, several individuals may occupy the same role, especially for large or critical purchases. It is not unusual for a variety of members of the organization to serve as influencers, since these roles are not normally fixed and formal. Roles change as the purchase decision changes.

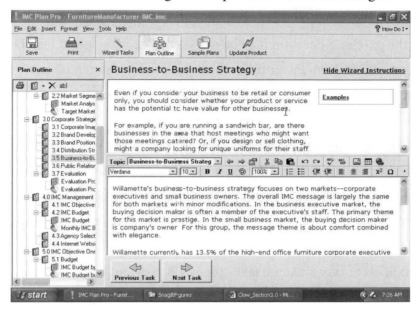

Figure 3.5 — Many businesses will also have other businesses as customers so thinking about your business strategy here will help you when you get to Section 7.0 of the IMC Plan.

Types of Business-to-Business Purchases

Each business' buying behavior process is unique. Every company has its own management style, marketing program, and individuals that participate in buying decisions. Salespeople calling on a business must be able to locate members of the buying center and understand their roles in the process. Creatives designing brochures and ads must decide which member of the buying center will be targeted. This makes selling to other businesses a complex task. Buying situations can usually be described using three categories: straight re-buy, modified re-buy, or a new task purchase.

A *straight re-buy* occurs when the firm has previously chosen a vendor and wishes to re-order. This tends to be a routine process. Only one or a few members of the buying center are involved. Often the purchasing agent (buyer) and the users of the product are the only persons aware of a re-buy order. The user's role in this purchase situation is to ask the buyer to replenish the supply. Contact is then made with the supplier and an order is placed. The buyer is not likely to evaluate any new alternatives or information. Often orders are placed electronically.

A *modified re-buy* occurs in a repurchase situation in which the buying team will consider and evaluate new alternatives, comparing them to the previous choice. A modified re-buy purchase occurs in four situations. First, when the company buyers are dissatisfied with a current vendor, they may look for new options. The greater the level of dissatisfaction, the greater will be the enticement to seek out new possibilities.

Second, when a new company offers what is perceived by a member of the buying center to be a better buy, the purchase decision may be revisited. The new option may be a superior quality product or one offered at a lower price. Also, the terms of purchase may be more attractive with a different company. When the dependability of a new vendor is perceived superior to the current vendor, the company may reconsider its previous choice.

A third reason situation in which a modified re-buy occurs is at end of a contractual agreement with a vendor. Many companies, as dictated by corporate policy, ask for bids each time a contract is written. This is true in many governmental and institutional organizations. The amount of time spent on the buying process depends on a comparison between the company's current vendor with other potential vendors.

The last modified re-buy situation takes place when a company purchases a good or service with which they have only limited or infrequent experience. For example, a company that purchases delivery trucks every five to seven years would probably make a modified re-buy, because many factors change over that amount of time. Prices, product features, and vendors (truck dealerships) change rapidly. Further, in most cases, the composition of the buying group will be different.

In general, modified re-buys occur when someone in the buying center believes it is worth re-evaluating vendors based on new information. The decision to reconsider will depend on the buying center individual's ability to influence other members of the group. Company policies may also dictate modified re-buy procedures.

In *new task* purchasing situations, the company is buying a good or service for the first time. The purchase is one with which members of the buying center have no experience. This type of purchase requires greater inputs from many sources. A considerable amount of time is spent gathering information and evaluating vendors. In many cases, vendors are asked to assist in identifying the specifications that will be required.

In developing a business-to-business strategy for your IMC plan, first consider the buying center and which members of the buying center will be approached. Also note the type of buying situation that exits. If a company already has a contract with a vendor, you are looking at a modified re-buy situation. Part of your strategy must be to find a way of getting your information past the gatekeepers to the users, influencers, or deciders.

Even when the business is primarily oriented to retail outlets or consumers, it is still possible to adapt the good or service to other businesses. For example, a sandwich bar can also cater lunches for local businesses. Or, if you design or sell clothing, there may be a nearby company looking for unique uniforms. Next is the business-to-business strategy for Willamette Furniture. B-to-B sales account for a great deal of Willamette's revenues.

3.5 Business-to-Business Strategy

Willamette's business-to-business strategy focuses on two markets--corporate executives and small business owners. The overall IMC message is largely the same for both markets with minor modifications. In the business executive market, the buying decision maker is often a member of the executive's staff. The primary theme for this market is prestige. In the small business market, the buying decision maker is normally the company's owner. For this group, the message theme is about comfort combined with elegance.

Sales to small businesses accounted for 30% of total company revenues last year. We believe small business represent a major opportunity market, especially for direct marketing. While the catalog will be the primary direct marketing tool, a large portion of this market can be reached through online marketing. It is relatively easy to purchase mailing lists and email addresses of small business owners. Consequently, the move into direct marketing to this segment should also be relative easy to implement.

The business-to-business segments of Willamette's business account for a large percentage of total company revenues. We can increase our market share in the corporate executive segment gradually. However, it is in the small business market that we feel the fastest growth can occur and that we can increase our market substantially with a concentrated IMC approach.

Section 3.6   Public Relations Strategy

Public relations is not like other marketing functions. The marketing department normally concentrates on customers and the channel members. In contrast, the public relations department focuses on a variety of internal and external stakeholders. These include employees, stockholders, public interest groups, the government, and society as a whole. Consequently, in many organizations the public relations department is separate from the marketing department. The two normally cooperate with and consult each other, yet each has a separate role to perform. There are three key public relations functions:

- Monitor internal and external publics.
- Provide positive information to each public that reinforces the IMC Plan.
- React quickly to any negative publicity or events that may negatively impact the IMC Plan.

The first major strategic decision to be made is who will handle public relations activities. Most firms have an internal public relations officer or department. Others hire public relations firms to handle either special projects or all public relations functions. Still, even when a public relations agency is retained, a firm normally places someone in charge of internal public relations, since most public relations firms deal only with external publics.

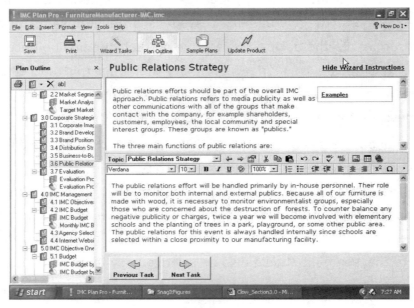

Figure 3.6 — Information about the public relations firm and strategy that will be used is placed in this section of your plan.

When a public relations firm is used, the agency's personnel must be familiar with your IMC plan. The public relations company can work on ideas that reinforce the plan. Special events, sponsorships, special events, cause-related activities, and news releases should be developed to strengthen the "one voice" needed to build a successful IMC program. Hiring a public relations firm is especially critical if you plan to develop any type of sponsorship program.

In this section of your IMC plan, discuss what will the primary role of your public relations group. The approach may be to maintain a constant image of community involvement or to enhance an image of environmental consciousness. Another is to reinforce an image of innovation and creativity. Here are some questions that may help you in developing the public relations strategy:

- How will you generate positive publicity about your company and products?
- How will you supplement your advertising effort with public relations?
- Has there been any negative publicity that the company should address? What is the plan for overcoming this negative publicity?

The Willamette Furniture public relations strategy is shown next. Notice that it mentions both who will be in charge and some of the activities the company will pursue. These activities are designed to generate positive publicity for the firm.

3.6 Public Relations Strategy

Our public relations efforts will be handled primarily by in-house personnel. They will monitor both internal and external publics. They will also be in charge of public relations events and sponsorship programs.

Our furniture is made with wood. This makes it necessary to monitor environmentalist groups, especially those who are concerned about the destruction of forests. To counter any negative publicity or charges, twice a year we will become involved with elementary schools and the planting of trees in a park, playground, or some other public area. Publicity for these events should be generated internally. The schools to be contacted are those in close proximity to our manufacturing facility.

We will also create annual sponsorship programs. An outside public relations firm may be used to develop these programs The theme of each year's sponsorship program will be based events planned for our area. Careful tie-ins will be made between any group that is sponsored with our products. Many of these events will be targeted at members of the business community, such as local job fairs, or community business expos.

Section 3.7 Evaluation

No IMC strategy section is complete without choosing methods of evaluation. The methods chosen should match the objectives being measured. For example, if the objective of an advertising campaign is to increase customer interest in and recall of a brand, then the level of customer awareness should be measured. Normally this means the marketing team will measure awareness before and after the ads are run. This procedure is commonly known as pre- and post-test analysis. To complete this section of your IMC plan, you need to consider several topics, including: (1) the IMC objectives your company wishes to reach, (2) the times to evaluate, (3) the methods of evaluation, and (4) complications that can disrupt evaluation.

Evaluation Objectives

Several levels of analysis should be identified when preparing objectives for an IMC program. They include:

- Short term outcomes (sales, redemption rates)
- Long term results (brand awareness, brand loyalty or equity)
- Product-specific awareness
- Awareness of the overall company
- Affective responses (liking the company and a positive brand image)

A company with low brand awareness may be most interested in visibility and memorability objectives. At the same time, a marketing program designed to boost brand awareness may not result in immediate sales. Remember, creating objectives for a sales promotion campaign featuring coupons using sales figures is easier to do then designing measuring objectives for an advertising campaign on television. Consequently, promotions objectives and the methods used to evaluate them should include both mental and behavioral elements.

The evaluation methodology must match the objectives of your IMC Plan. Therefore, this section of your IMC plan should be completed along with the IMC objectives you will first place in Section 4.1.

When To Evaluate

Evaluation or testing of advertising communications can occur at any stage of the development process, even before the ad is ever produced. Testing normally involves soliciting the opinions of both experts and "regular" people.

One typical time to begin measurement is when the design stage has been completed but prior to development. A television ad may be produced using a storyboard. A storyboard is a series of still photographs or sketches that outline the structure of the ad. Reactions to the approach being taken and primary message can be solicited during this stage.

After a commercial is produced, experimental tests can be used to evaluate the effect. At that point, a group of consumers can be invited to watch the ad in a theater-type setting. The test ad is placed in a group of ads. Viewers are then asked to evaluate all of the ads (including the test ad) to see if it had the desired effect.

Before launching an advertising campaign, the agency may show the ad in a test market area. Several tools can then be used to measure the quality and impact of the ad. These instruments will be presented next.

The final place where evaluation can occur is after the marketing communication has been used. Information collected at this time helps the company's leaders and the advertising agency to assess what worked and what didn't. The findings are then used in the development of future marketing campaigns.

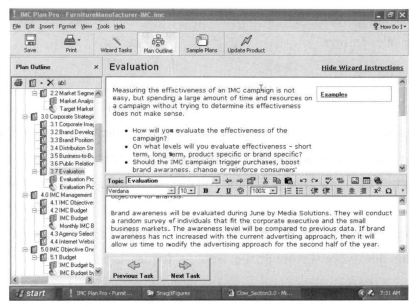

Figure 3.7 — Thinking about how and when you will evaluate your IMC Plan is critical to long-term success.

Evaluation Methods

Several methods can be used to evaluate the message content of an advertisement or marketing communication piece. While most of the methods deal with the verbal or written components of the communication piece, peripheral cues are also important and should be part of the message evaluation. These methods include:

- Concept testing
- Copytesting
- Recall tests
- Recognition tests
- Attitude and opinion tests
- Emotional reaction tests
- Physiological arousal tests
- Persuasion tests

While these techniques provide valuable insights into what people think and feel, there are some who contend that the only valid evaluation criterion of an IMC plan should be actual sales. To these critics it is less important for an ad to be well-liked. If an ad does not increase sales, then it is not an effective ad. The same type of argument is often presented regarding the other marketing communication tools such as sales promotions, trade promotions, personal selling, and direct marketing. There is some validity to this viewpoint; however, not all communication objectives can be measured using sales figures.

Complications

In general, careful planning prior to initiating an advertising or IMC program makes evaluation of the campaign easier and more accurate. At the same time, the evaluation of a specific advertisement is difficult, because many factors may affect the outcome being measured. Three factors that make quality assessment more complex are (1) uncontrollable circumstances, (2) competitive reactions, and (3) the timing of presentation.

Many circumstances are simply *uncontrollable*. For instance, a retailer may run a series of newspaper and radio ads to boost store traffic. In order to measure the impact of the ads, the retailer keeps records of store traffic before, during, and after the ad campaign. Unfortunately, the traffic count may be affected by factors as simple as the weather. If it rains for two days, the traffic count will probably be lower. An unforeseen event, such as the season finale of a major television series, or a special program (commencement, all-school play) at the local high school could have impact. Many extraneous factors can affect the results of a marketing program. Thus, in reviewing results, these factors should be kept in mind.

A company's chief *competitor* can also affect the measurement of effectiveness. The competitor may run a special sale during the same time period. This would also affect traffic. A competitor may run advertisements designed to blunt the influence of your campaign. Marketing programs do not happen in a vacuum. You must be aware of how the competition has tried to influence consumers while you are trying to reach them.

Also assessing the effectiveness of an ad can be affected by the *date or time* the advertisement appeared. Different seasons (Christmas, summer, back-to-school) affect interest in and perceptions of marketing messages. The marketing team should be aware of timing. For example, the dates a magazine reaches newsstands and when subscribers receive copies at home are important items used in evaluating magazine ads.

More importantly, perhaps, is to remember that the analysis of one advertising campaign or promotions program may not assess the impact on the larger company image. For example, even though store traffic was low, the ad may have been recalled and stored in the buyer's long term memory. At some future point this may make a difference. Conversely, the same ad may have been awkward or in some way offensive and the store owner may believe the weather affected the outcome instead of a poor advertising design. Consequently, company leaders must be reminded to consider both short term consequences and long term implications when overall IMC programs are being assessed.

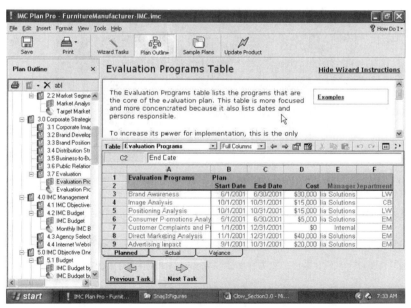

Figure 3.8 — You may not be able to actually complete this table of what you will evaluate, when it will be evaluated, and who will evaluate it until you have completed more of your IMC Plan.

As you can see, measuring the effectiveness of an IMC campaign is not easy. Still, spending large amounts of time and resources on a campaign without trying to determine its effectiveness does not make sense. To guide you in writing this section, some questions that you might address include:

- How will you evaluate the effectiveness of your objectives?
- On what levels will you evaluate effectiveness - short term, long term, product specific or brand specific?
- Should this IMC campaign trigger purchases, boost brand awareness, change or reinforce consumers' image of your company or product?
- Will your evaluation be continuous, or on the basis of specific ads, promotions and PR pushes?
- Will you test ads and promotions before they are fully launched? If so, at what stage of the ad or promotion development will you test?
- How and when will you test the various components of your IMC Plan such as your direct marketing campaign, your frequency program, and your consumer promotions?

The goal of this section of your IMC plan is to spell out marketing objects along with how you will evaluate the results. Here is the evaluation strategy for Willamette Furniture.

3.7 Evaluation

Evaluations of our IMC Plan will be conducted internally and by Media Solutions. Our marketing objectives and methods of evaluation are summarized below.

Brand awareness will be evaluated during June by Media Solutions. A random survey of individuals that fit the three different target markets will be conducted. The awareness level will be collected annually and compared to previous data. If brand awareness has not increased with the current advertising approach, then it will allow us time to modify our advertising approach for the second half of the year.

The **positioning analysis** will be conducted October. If the position does not fit the projected position of the firm, it will allow us to modify our IMC campaign for the next calendar year.

The **effectiveness of our consumer promotions** will be measured during May and June.

Customer complaints and product returns will be measured and monitored on a continual basis. We will not be able to position ourselves in this sector unless our production facility delivers on what we promise. All customer complaints or product returns will be forwarded to our marketing department for recording and analysis.

We will have Media Solutions conduct an **advertising impact** study for us beginning September 1st and running through October 31st. This evaluation should provide information concerning how influential advertising campaign has been. We will be using attitude and opinion tests. We especially want to see if our slogan "For the Best" is understood and if it positively impacts the image of our company and its products.

Since we will be using **trade promotions** to push our product through the channel, we want to measure the impact of the trade contests, trade incentives, vendor support programs, trade shows, and specialty advertising. This evaluation will take place in April of each year.

Personal selling will be critical for achieving our 2nd and 3rd IMC objectives so evaluation of our personal selling will take place in February and March. We want to measure the satisfaction level of our business customers and distribution channel members. We will also examine sales call effectiveness.

The **direct marketing program** will be evaluated in November and December. This will allow time to see the impact of the direct mailings. It will also give time to evaluate the effectiveness of the online direct marketing program. Because the direct marketing campaign is so vital to our IMC campaign's success, Media Solutions will be charged with the responsibility of evaluating the success of these efforts.

Evaluation Programs	Plan Start Date	End Date	Cost	Manager	Dept.
Brand Awareness	6/1/2005	6/30/2005	$30,000	Media Solutions	LW
Image Analysis	10/1/2005	10/31/2005	$15,000	Media Solutions	CB
Positioning Analysis	10/1/2005	10/31/2005	$15,000	Media Solutions	LW
Consumer Promotions Analysis	5/1/2005	6/30/2005	$5,000	Media Solutions	EM
Customer Complaints and Product Returns	1/1/2005	12/31/2005	$0	Internal	EM
Advertising Impact	9/1/2005	10/31/2005	$20,000	Media Solutions	EM
Trade Promotions Analysis	4/1/2005	4/20/2005	$2,000	Media Solutions	EM
Analysis of Personal Selling Effectiveness	2/1/2005	3/31/2005	$0	Media Solutions	EM
Direct Marketing Analysis	11/1/2005	12/31/2005	$20,000	Media Solutions	EM
Totals			$107,000		

Table 3.1 — Consumer Evaluation Programs

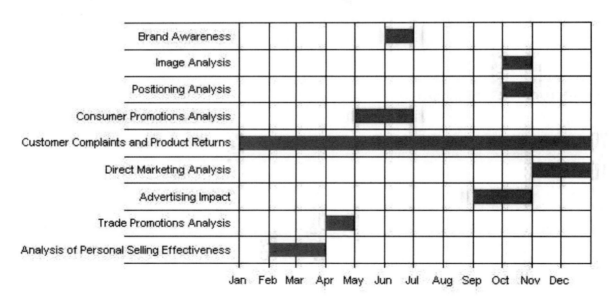

Figure 3.9 — Consumer Evaluation Programs (Graph)

Section 4
IMC Management

One of the most important elements in an IMC plan is stating the marketing objectives your company would like to reach. These objectives are generated as part of the promotions opportunity analysis performed in Section 2.0 combined with the corporate strategies defined in Section 3.0. Once the overall IMC objectives are clearly stated, other parts of the IMC program can be finalized. Section 4.0 of the IMC Plan Pro contains four parts: (1) stating the marketing objectives, (2) creating an overall IMC budget, (3) selecting an advertising agency, and (4) developing a Web site. Your IMC plan covers these items in sections 4.1, 4.2, 4.3, and 4.4.

Section 4.0

Section 4.0 begins with a summary paragraph addressing the key management issues present in your IMC campaign. The summary should identify the main goals you want to accomplish. Also, spell out how these goals are related to the current marketing campaign. It helps to write a brief rationale about the direction the company is headed along with the IMC budget needed to get there. Here is the IMC Management Statement for Willamette Furniture.

4.0 IMC Management

Past sales figures indicate that we have successfully reached our target market segments; exclusive retail stores and direct sales to other businesses. We expect continued success in the future. To achieve this success, we will build our current market segments and supplement those efforts with a more aggressive direct marketing program

The budget for our IMC program for next year will be $7,000,000. The $7,000,000 will be allocated as follows:

The largest percentage, 35.7%, of the IMC budget will be used to maintain our market share in the corporate executive market. There is intense competition in this market, which makes it vital to continue to emphasize this element of the IMC plan.

To increase market share in the small business market, 26.4% of the IMC budget, or $1.85 million, will be used for that purpose. This is a higher percentage of sales than the industry average. We believe that these additional expenditures are necessary in order to increase our current 12% market share.

The largest budget increase will go to the home office segment. This is a market that no other company has ever aggressively pursued. This is where our direct marketing program is most important. A concentrated effort aimed at the top 20% of this market should yield substantial sales. Consequently, $2.25 million (22.7% of sales in this market) of our IMC budget is allocated to this market. This represents 13.7% of the total IMC budget. As a result, we anticipate operating a loss in this market during the next year. If the current market share of 8% can be increased substantially, then the investment will be beneficial in the long term.

Section 4.1 IMC Objectives

The process of defining and establishing communications objectives is a crucial element of the Integrated Marketing Communications Plan. Without clearly specified objectives, a company can quickly drift off course or lose its focus. IMC objectives continually remind members of the organization of the direction that the marketing team is taking.

In this section of the IMC plan, your specific overall IMC objectives are identified. These objectives should result from the promotions opportunity analysis you conducted in Section 2.0. The objectives lead to selection of communication methodologies and tools. They also provide the marketing creatives with the primary information needed to design the actual advertisements and related marketing materials. Common IMC objectives include:

- Develop brand awareness
- Increase category demand
- Change customer beliefs or attitudes
- Enhance purchase actions
- Encourage repeat purchases
- Build customer traffic

- Enhance firm image
- Increase market share
- Increase sales
- Reinforce purchase decisions

Your IMC may be oriented toward a single objective. It is possible, however, for a program to accomplish more than one goal at a time. For example, a local restaurant in Florida could give a 10 percent discount to its frequent diner members from May through October. The primary goal of this promotion is to increase customer traffic at its various restaurants during the off-season. The catch to the discount, however, could be it can only be used at one of the company's other restaurants, not the restaurant where the discount was issued. This would encourage customers to visit other locations in the area. As the discounts accumulate they encourage repeat purchases. Thus, a program designed to build customer traffic also reinforced purchase decisions and encourages purchases at other locations.

Numerous logical combinations of IMC objectives are possible. These can be achieved using logically-linked marketing tactics. For example, advertising is an excellent means of developing brand awareness and enhancing a brand's image. Increasing sales can be accomplished using price changes, contests, or coupons. The key is to match the objective to the medium and the message.

Think about what you want to accomplish as you prepare your IMC goals. You may want to put something into the consumer's mind, change attitudes, or persuade specific consumers to act. When the company's potential customers do not know about its product or service, one objective will be to increase awareness. When customers are aware of the product, but know little about it, the objective may be to build knowledge. When customers know about your products, you may try to get them to like your product and your company more. Potential customers that like your product but still buy the competition's product require additional information. The objective may be to persuade them of the superiority or uniqueness of your offering. Some customers prefer your product but have not gotten around to buying it. Then the objective is to inspire them to take the last step and make the purchase.

Three communications objectives should be developed as part of Section 4.0. The first is for the consumer market. It becomes the basis of Section 5.0 of this plan. The second communication objective is for the distribution channel. It is the basis of Section 6.0. The third communications objective is for the business-to-business market. It will be the basis for Section

7.0. Each objective is based on the company's current position in that particular market and what you would like to accomplish with this IMC Plan.

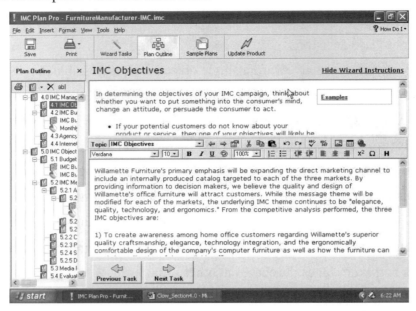

Figure 4.1 — The objectives for your IMC Plan should be listed in Section 4.1.

The objectives for Willamette Furniture are stated below. For the consumer market, the opportunity analysis revealed that home office customers were not highly aware of Willamette and what the company has to offer. Therefore, the objective for the consumer market is to create awareness.

The situation with the distribution channel is different. Channel members had an awareness of the Willamette brand, but did not push the brand effectively. The company is setting two objectives for the distribution channel. The first is to persuade channel members to stock the Willamette brand. The second is to push the Willamette brand through providing their customers with information about Willamette line of office furniture.

For the business-to-business market, the promotions opportunity analysis indicated limited awareness of the Willamette brand. Willamette could choose an objective of increasing awareness or of moving the market to the next step, knowledge. Willamette's marketing team believes that the awareness campaign used for the consumer market will spill over to this market. They also believe that a sufficient number of businesses were aware enough about the brand that it is possible to move marketing communications to the next level. This step is to inform business customers about Willamette's superior quality, craftsmanship, elegance, technology integration, and ergonomically comfortable design.

4.1 IMC Objectives

Willamette Furniture's primary emphasis will be expanding the direct marketing channel to using an internally produced catalog targeted to each of the three markets. By providing information to decision makers, we believe the quality and design of Willamette's office furniture will attract customers. While the message theme will be modified for each of the markets, the underlying IMC theme continues to be "elegance, quality, technology, and ergonomics." From the competitive analysis performed, the three IMC objectives are:

1) To **create awareness** among home office customers. They should find out about Willamette's superior quality craftsmanship, elegance, technology integration, and the ergonomically comfortable design of the company's computer furniture as well as how the furniture can maximize utilization of the available office space.

2) To **persuade** channel members such as wholesalers, office furniture dealers, office designers, office furniture catalogers, and retail outlets to carry the catalog brand and provide information to potential customers.

3) To **inform** the office staff members close to corporate executives about Willamette's superior quality craftsmanship, elegance, technology integration, and ergonomically comfortable design in the company's computer furniture as well as how this furniture provides prestige for executives. Also, to inform small business owners about these same features and how they create comfort and quality for these individuals.

Section 4.2 IMC Budget

Marketing costs money. Marketing money should be spent wisely. This makes budgeting a central part of any IMC plan. Several methods are used by companies to develop their IMC budgets. They include (1) the percentage of sales method, (2) the meet the competition approach, (3) the "what we can afford" budget, and (4) the objective and task approach.

A widely-used approach to budgeting is *percentage of sales* method. Companies that use this method prepare communications budgets for coming years based on either: (1) sales from the previous year or (2) anticipated sales for the next year. The major reason for using this format is simplicity. A percentage of sales budget is relatively easy to prepare.

The percentage of sales approach is not perfect. One problem is that it tends to change in the opposite direction of what may be needed. That is, when sales go up, so does the communications budget. When sales decline, the communications budget also declines. In most cases, the communication budget should be the opposite. It should be increased during periods of declining sales to help reverse the trend. During growth periods the communication budget may not need to be increased. The second major disadvantage of this method is that it does not allocate money for special needs or to combat competitive pressures.

A second budgeting approach is the *meet-the-competition* method. The primary goal of this form of budgeting is to prevent the loss of market share. It is often used in highly competitive markets where rivalries between competitors are intense. The potential drawback to meet-the-competition budgeting is that marketing dollars may not be spent efficiently. Matching the competition's spending does not guarantee success--market share can still be lost.

The third type of budgeting is called *"what we can afford."* The technique sets the marketing budget after all of the company's other budgets have been determined. Money is allocated based on what the company leaders feel they can afford. This method is often used by newer and smaller companies with limited finances.

The final form of budgeting is called the *objective and task* method. To prepare this type of communications budget, management first lists all of the objectives they intend to pursue during the year. Next, the cost of accomplishing each objective is calculated. The communications budget is the cumulative sum of the estimated costs for all objectives.

The objective and task method is probably the best method of budgeting. Many marketing experts note that it relates dollar costs to achieving specific objectives. Unfortunately, it is the least used, primarily because it takes longer to prepare than many of the other approaches. For a company such as Procter & Gamble offering hundreds of products, producing a budget based on objectives for each brand and product category would take many of hours, and other methods are faster and simpler.

Normally, about 25% of a communications budget is used for advertising. Trade promotions receive about 50%, and consumer promotions are given on average about 25%. These percentages vary considerably from industry to industry, but the numbers do give you some idea of current business practice. Consumer product manufacturers spend more on trade promotions directed toward retailers while service companies tend to spend more on media advertising.

Budgets also vary by product types as well. For example, for dolls and stuffed toys, the average expenditure on media advertising as a percentage of sales is about 15%; while for bakery products expenditures on media advertising represent only 3% of sales.

Your next step in preparing an IMC plan is creating an overall marketing communications budget. Look at what was spent last year and in previous years. Investigate your primary competitors and what they are spending. Most importantly, examine the goals for this IMC Plan. Based on this information, an overall IMC budget can be developed.

Once you have created an overall IMC budget, decide how much to allocate to the consumer market, the distribution channel, and the business-to-business market. This information will be used in the individual budgets found in Sections 5.1, 6.1, and 7.1.

Please note that the IMC Budget Table in this section of your IMC Plan is not built here. It will be developed after you work out budgets in each section. The numbers that are listed for the Consumer Budget in this table are derived from the IMC Objective One budget from Section 5.1. The same is true for the Distribution Channel budget and the Business-to-Business budget. The numbers in this table come from the budgets you develop in Sections 6.1, and 7.1, respectively. The same is true for the bar chart. The total monthly expenditures shown in the graph are derived from the budgets you develop in later sections. As long as you do not change any of the formulas in the IMC Budge table found in Section 4.2 on your IMC Plan Pro, you do not have to enter any budgetary numbers into the table. As you can see, this information has already been finalized for the Willamette Company.

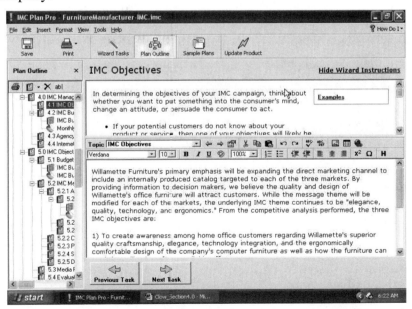

Figure 4.2 — The budget figures in this table in Section 4.1 are derived from other parts of the IMC Plan Pro software.

4.2 IMC Budget

Willamette Furniture has three distinct markets to pursue: corporate executives, small business owners, and home offices which may be business offices or personal offices. The IMC $7 million budget will be distributed as follows:

- IMC Objective 1: $ 2,250,000
- IMC Objective 2: $ 1,040,000
- IMC Objective 3: $ 3,710,000

IMC Objective 1 addresses the needs of the home office market, in which we have only 8% share. The potential exists to substantially increase our market share. Therefore, 32.14% of the IMC budget is allocated to this objective.

IMC Objective 2 addresses the needs of the channel of distribution. Approximately 14.8% of the budget will be used to maintain current channel relationships and to expand to additional furniture dealers and office designers.

IMC Objective 3 deals with the business-to-business aspect of our marketing program. This includes both the corporate executive market and the small business market. We will achieve our objectives in this market by using 53% of the IMC funds here. While there will be some overlap in the communication tools used for these two markets, each will have a tailor-made message attached to the overall IMC theme.

IMC Budget	2001	2002	2003	2004	2005
Consumer	$2,250,000	$2,250,000	$2,279,000	$2,378,000	$2,458,000
Distribution Channel	$1,038,000	$1,180,000	$1,230,000	$1,280,000	$1,330,000
Business-to-Business	$3,710,000	$3,865,000	$4,015,000	$4,170,000	$4,290,000
Total Budget	$6,998,000	$7,295,000	$7,524,000	$7,828,000	$8,078,000

Table 4.1 — IMC Budget.

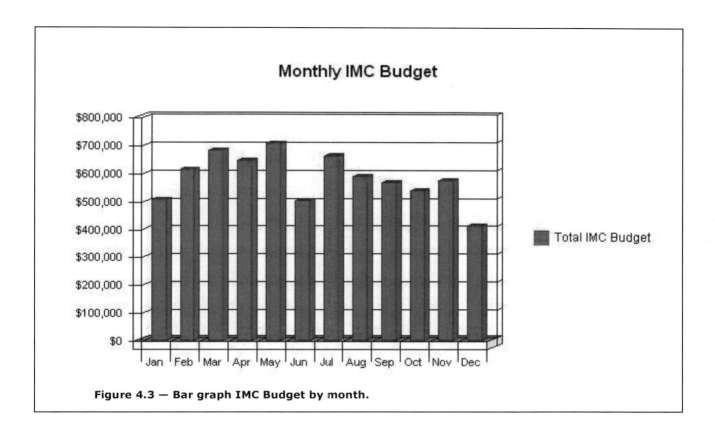

Figure 4.3 — Bar graph IMC Budget by month.

Section 4.3 Agency Selection

Before you create an actual advertising program, company leaders must choose between an in-house advertising group and an external advertising agency. Many larger-sized organizations have begun to house integrated communications and advertising programs within internal departments. The reasoning is that internal members of the organization have a better sense of the company's mission and message. These firms hire a few key marketing and advertising experts to develop effective advertising programs. The marketing team outsources some of the functions, such as the writing, filming or recording, and editing the actual advertisement in addition to planning and purchasing media time (on television and radio) and space (in magazines, newspapers, and on billboards).

The disadvantage to such an internal communications and advertising department is that the company can go "stale" in its marketing efforts and may fail to recognize other promotional or advertising opportunities. The department may also lack the expertise to carry out all of the necessary functions. Instead, the tendency may be to cut costs in developing ads rather than taking advantage of the knowledge and expertise that advertising agencies have to offer. This is especially true in the international arena, where a firm probably lacks the necessary understanding of language, customs, as well as key buyer behaviors in target markets.

In making the decision to use an external agency or in-house department, a firm should consider the following critical issues:

1) The size of the account
2) Advertising budget
3) Advertising expertise
4) The complexity of the product being sold
5) Creativity of the internal staff

Concerning the account size, a small account is not usually attractive to an advertising agency, because they see little opportunity for profit. Also, smaller accounts are less economically sound for the agency, because more money must be spent on production of advertisements rather than purchasing media time or space. A good rule of thumb is called the 75/15/10 breakdown. That is, 75% of the money should be used to buy media time or space, 15% should go to the agency for the creative work, and 10% should be spent on the actual production of the ad. For smaller accounts, the breakdown may be more like 25/40/35, where 75% of the funds go to the agency for creative and production work, and only 25% is spent on media purchases. The rule of thumb is that unless 75% of the company's advertising budget can be spent on media purchases, it may be wiser to do the work either in-house or to develop contracts with smaller ad firms or freelancers to prepare various aspects of the advertising campaign. Remember that an external agency carries greater advertising and creative expertise. Creatives working for an in-house advertising department are paid by the company instead of an independent ad agency. Many times it is more difficult for in-house creatives to remain unbiased and to ignore the influences of others in the organization who may not fully understand the artistic aspects of advertising. The exception is highly complex products. Agency members may have a difficult time understanding more complicated products. To get them to understand often requires a considerable of time. For complex products, in-house departments may work best. For generic or more standard and simple products, ad agencies may have more to offer.

When the decision is made to utilize an external advertising agency, the company is committing substantial resources to the goal of expanding its audience. A variety of options are available when hiring an advertising agency. All sizes and types of advertising agencies exist. At one end of the spectrum are the highly specialized, boutique-type agencies which offer only one specialized service (e.g., making television ads), or that serve one particular type of client, such as

Native Americans. At the other end of the spectrum are the full service agencies providing all types of advertising services as well as advice and assistance in working with the other components of the IMC model, such as sales and trade promotions, direct marketing programs, and public relations events.

In addition to advertising agencies, there are other closely associated types of firms. These include media service companies who negotiate and purchase media packages for (called "media buys") for companies. There are also direct marketing agencies who can handle every aspect of a direct marketing campaign, either through telephone orders (800 numbers), Internet programs, or by direct mail. Some companies focus on either sales promotions or trade promotions or both. These companies assist contests, sweepstakes, and other types of promotions. Public relations firms are experts in helping companies and individuals develop positive public images, and are also called in for damage control when negative publicity arises. These activities may be rendered by in-house members of the organization, just as advertising and IMC programs can be performed by an in-house marketing department. In both instances, company leaders must decide how they can effectively and efficiently complete these key marketing activities.

The decision to retain an advertising agency is largely based on the belief that the agency can provide services and assistance which will give the client firm an advantage in the marketplace. A high quality advertising agency can help a firm create and build the type of strong image and brand name that is critical for survival in the 21st century. A strong brand name strengthens both consumer and business-to-business preferences for products. This, in turn results in greater sales, lower marketing costs, and allows the producer to charge a price premium. Therefore, finding an advertising agency that can create both a strong brand name and increase brand sales is important for long-run success.

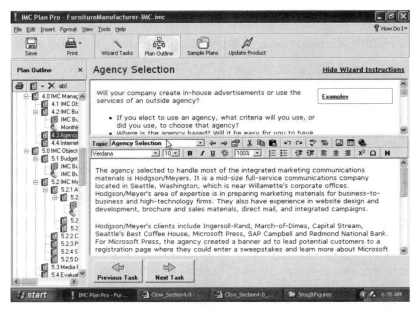

Figure 4.4 — In this section is information about the advertising agency that is selected and why it was chosen.

Choosing the advertising agency that best suits a company requires careful planning. In making this selection, the following steps should be followed:

1) Identify and prioritize corporate goals
2) Develop agency selection criteria and the process that will be used
3) Screen initial candidates based on credentials, size, capabilities, relevant experience, and conflict of interests
4) Request client references
5) Request a written and oral presentation

The marketing team should *identify and prioritize corporate goals* before making contact with an advertising agency. The goals should guide the company's leaders, the agency account executive, and the advertising creative. Each should be "on the same page" as preparation of the advertising campaign unfolds. Without clearly understood goals, it is more difficult to choose an agency. This is because there is no direction about what to accomplish. Clear goals help ensure a good fit between the company and the agency which is eventually chosen.

The second step in selecting an agency is to finalize the process and *refine the criteria* to be used. Even firms with experience in selecting agencies must establish the process and criteria in advance. The idea is to reduce biases that may enter into the decision process. Emotions and other feelings can lead to decisions that are not in the best interests of the company. While it is important to have a good chemistry between the agency and the firm, this aspect of the choice should come later in the process, after the list has been narrowed down to two or three agencies.

Common factors used as part of the initial screening process include agency size, relevant experience, conflicts of interest, creative ability, production capabilities, and media purchasing capabilities.

The *size of the agency* is important, especially as it compares to the size of the company hiring the agency. If a large firm were to hire a small agency, the small agency may be overwhelmed by the account. A small firm hiring a large agency may find that their account might be lost or they could be treated as being insignificant. A good rule of thumb to follow regarding the size of the agency is that the account should be large enough for the agency that it is important to them but small enough that, if lost, the agency would not be badly affected. *Relevant experience in an industry* is a second evaluation criterion that companies use. There is a built-in advantage when an agency has experience in a given industry. The agency team understands the client firm, its customers, and the structure of the marketing channel. At the same time, it is important to be certain the agency does not have any conflicts of interest. An advertising firm that has been hired by one manufacturer of tires would experience a conflict of interest if they were hired by another tire company. Further, the agency should have relevant experience without representing a competitor. Such experience may be gained when an agency sells a related product or works for similar firm that operates in a different industry. For example, if an agency has a manufacturer of automobile batteries as a client, this experience would be relevant to selling automobile tires. The agency should have experience with the business-to-business side of the market, so that retailers, wholesalers, and any other channel party are considered in the marketing and advertising of the product.

The initial screening process includes an investigation into each agency's *creative reputation* and *capabilities.* One method of judging an agency's creativity is by asking for a list of awards the company has received. Although awards do not always translate into effective advertisements, in most cases there a strong relationship exists between winning awards and writing effective ads. Most creative awards are given by peers. As a result, they are good indicators of what others think of the agency's creative efforts. Assessing creative capabilities would be very important when developing advertising campaigns for foreign countries where the firm has limited experience.

Production capabilities and *media purchasing capabilities* of the agencies are also examined. The information is gathered in order to be sure that the agency has the necessary capabilities. A firm seeking an agency which can both produce the television commercial and buy media time should check on these items as part of the initial screening process. Media buying skills are important.

Once the initial screening has been completed, it is time to *request references* from those agencies that are still in the running for the contract. Most agencies are willing to provide lists of their best customers to serve as references. A good strategy the company can use is to obtain references of firms that have similar needs. Also, when possible, it helps to obtain names of companies who were former clients of the agency. Finding out why they switched can be valuable information. Often changes are made for legitimate reasons. Discovering an agency's client retention rate helps reveal how effective they have been in working with various clients.

The final step in the selection process is to request an *oral and written presentation* by the finalists. The agency should be willing to provide a formal presentation addressing a specific problem, situation, or set of questions. These presentations reveal how each agency would deal with specific issues which arise as a campaign is prepared. This helps client companies to be certain the agency uses tactics and methods which are acceptable.

In this section of the IMC plan, discuss the decision to be used concerning using an external agency. Explain how the decision was made and criteria used. This should be followed by a discussion of the advertising selected and the work the agency will do for you. Here is the agency selection section for Willamette Furniture.

4.3 Agency Selection

The agency selected to handle most of the integrated marketing communications materials is Hodgson/Meyers. It is a mid-size full-service communications company located in Seattle, Washington, which is near Willamette's corporate offices. Hodgson/Meyer's area of expertise is in preparing marketing materials for business-to-business and high-technology firms. They also have experience in website design and development, brochure and sales materials, direct mail, and integrated campaigns.

Hodgson/Meyer's clients include Ingersoll-Rand, March-of-Dimes, Capital Stream, Seattle's Best Coffee House, Microsoft Press, SAP Campbell and Redmond National Bank. For Microsoft Press, the agency created a banner ad to lead potential customers to a registration page where they could enter a sweepstakes and learn more about Microsoft Press books. For Capital Stream, the agency prepared a new website. The one prepared by Hodgson/Meyers provided clear language, easy navigation, and an authoritative, professional image.

For SAP Campbell, Hodgson/Meyers designed an 18-month integrated campaign which included print ads, magazine inserts, Web redirects and surveys, direct mail pieces, digital video, flash product demos, and trade show promotions. This experience of integrating advertising with Web design and direct marketing programs was highly appealing to us. Hodgson/Meyers has the experience in business-to-business marketing as well as the Web design and the direct mail approach needed in our IMC campaign.

Media buying and public relations will be handled by separate firms with greater expertise than Hodgson/Meyers. For the public relations efforts, we will employ Firmani & Associates, a full-service public relations firm with over seven years of experience. For media buying, Media Solutions has been hired. Media Solutions will work closely with us and with our advertising agency to select the best media outlets. In addition to the media buys, Media Solutions will be conducting media research, both before and after our major campaigns. Media Solutions will assist in evaluation of the entire IMC campaign.

Section 4.4 Internet Web site

The design of a Web site should be guided by the IMC plan and the specific objectives the company wishes to accomplish. A flashy Web site designed to attract attention is created when the goal is advertising. Many firms use Web sites to promote individual products as well as the overall company. In this section of your IMC plan, you should examine the company's Web site as it relates to (1) advertising, (2) e-commerce, (3) sales support and customer service, and (4) public relations activities. Then it is possible to create an effective Internet program for the company.

Advertising is rarely presented by itself without being incorporated with other marketing functions. A company's advertising activities are almost always tied to the Web site. At the least, ads in other media mention the firm's web address. The Web site should display the same images and words that are found in company advertisements and other elements of the IMC program.

Also, the company can advertise on the Web on other sites. Sites connected to Google and others are common places to advertise. A company selling complementary or supplementary products may create links the firms selling related goods.

Many Web sites are designed to support *e-commerce* programs. E-commerce means selling goods on the Internet. It takes a variety of forms. A retail store can vend items to consumers through the Internet when there is no handy outlet nearby, or simply as a convenience for some shoppers. E-commerce can also be a retail operation that sells entirely on the Internet without any physical store or even inventory. Services are offered, deals are mediated, and products are shipped through this range of e-commerce operations.

E-commerce offers customers an alternative mode for making purchases. Not every customer uses the Internet, but many do. As time passes, more people will become more comfortable with Web site shopping. Without an e-commerce site, these customers may be lost to competing firms who have established retail online sites.

Remember that consumers make purchases at a retail store after first using the Internet to gather information. For example, a shopper may research stereos on the Internet and then go to the store with a list of "finalists." Another person may get on the Internet and find a fishing rod with a special set of features. Using the Internet store locator, the individual identifies the closest store offering the product to make the actual purchase. In that case, even though the customer did not make the purchase via e-commerce, he or she has used the Internet as part of the buying decision-making process. Consequently, the leaders of most established businesses know they must develop high quality e-commerce sites in order to remain competitive in the 21st century.

All e-commerce sites have three components. The first is some type of *catalog*. The catalog can vary from just a few items to a complex presentation of thousands of products. The nature of the firm's operation determines the type of catalog required. In every case, customers should be able to find the products of interest. Photos and product information are important in creating appealing online catalogs.

Second, each site must have some type of *shopping cart* to assist consumers as they select products. Again, the shopping cart can range from just checking a circle for an item when only a few products are offered to more complicated shopping carts that keeps records of multiple purchases.

Third, each site must establish some way for customers to make *payments* for the things they purchase. For consumers, this normally is a credit card system. For business-to-business operations payments are normally made through a voucher system. In other situations, a bill is generated or a computerized billing system is used so that the invoice goes directly to the buyer. In more trusting relationships, the invoice is added to the customer's records without a physical bill ever being mailed.

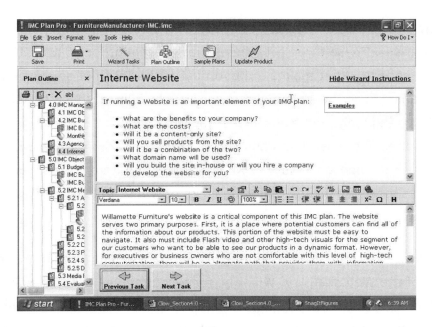

Figure 4.5 — By answering the questions in the instruction section, you will be able to develop your Web site strategy that is contained in Section 4.4 of the IMC Plan.

Some Web sites are more focused on *sales support*. In those instances, information about the products should be easily accessible through either a salesperson or a direct link from the Web page. These types of Web sites are used more routinely for the business-to-business customers rather than retail consumers. Effective sales support sites must be useful for engineers and other members of the buying center who need additional product information. The actual sale is normally made via a sales person. Then, the price and terms can be negotiated separately.

The *customer service* aspect of an Internet site provides a different function. The goal is to support the customer after the sale. In this instance, documentation and operating information are provided. Customers who have questions can use the e-mail function to obtain information or scroll through the FAQs, or Frequently Asked Questions people have about various items or services. Portions of these sites may be password protected in order to ensure that only customers who have purchased products can access certain information.

A Web site can be used to help create a positive *public relations* image. A company may place information any non-profit and philanthropic cause the firm supports on the Web site. Individuals not only see what the company is doing but also may be able to volunteer for or donate money to a cause. At times these sites are separate from the company's primary site. In others, a link within the site is developed. Preparing a public relations site may be used by a firm in order to react to bad publicity. This gives the firm the opportunity to refute a charge or to explain the company's side of the story.

In general, the Internet's greatest impact is on sales, marketing, and distribution systems of businesses. These three activities typically account for 20% to 30% of the final cost of a good or service. What makes the potential of the Internet so exciting is that e-commerce companies have the potential to save 10% to 20% of these costs. Instead of paying for packing, shipping, and transporting the product to a retail site, the firm has the option to send it directly to customers and can pocket the markup a retailer would receive. Also, the company can choose to mark down the price of an item. This saves customers money and entices more purchases. Shipping costs may also be charged to customers for e-commerce purchases, thus increasing profits.

Your Web site strategy is an essential element of the IMC Plan. In this section, discuss the role of the Web site play. Will it be for e-commerce? If so, does it supplement other forms of selling your products or is it the primary method of selling? What other functions will the Web site perform? Discuss each function of the Web site and how it will be designed to perform that function. Will you use internal staff to design the web site or will you hire someone else to do it for you, such as an advertising agency or a firm that specializes in Web site design? Next is the Internet Web site strategy for Willamette.

4.4 Internet Website

Willamette Furniture's Web site serves two primary purposes. First, it is a place where potential customers can find all of the information about our products. This portion of the website must be easy to navigate. It also must include Flash video and other high-tech visuals for the segment of our customers who want to be able to see our products in a dynamic format. For executives or business owners who are not comfortable with this level of high-tech computerization, there will be an alternate path that provides them with information.

The second purpose of the Web site is to take orders. It is our goal to ensure that the site reinforces Willamette's image of elegance, quality workmanship and ergonomics.

The primary purpose is to take orders rather than to generate sales. The site must be convenient and set up so that customers can easily place orders. In addition to ordering online, there will be human telephone operators available to talk with customers and take orders.

Hodgson/Meyers will help us accomplish these two goals for our Web site. The agency will work closely with our staff to redesign our Web site and then monitor its effectiveness. To ensure a complete assessment of success is being made, an outside firm, Media Solutions, will conduct a survey and an independent analysis of the website and our direct marketing approach.

Section 5
IMC Objective One: Consumers

Creating a positive influence on the attitudes and behaviors of consumers should be the ultimate goal of any integrated marketing communications program. Reaching consumers involves the use of several tools including advertising, consumer promotions, personal selling, sponsorship programs, and database programs. The relative use of each component of the IMC Program depends on your target market, your IMC objective, and your budget.

In this section, you are going to develop objectives for consumer markets. It takes more than advertising to reach these objectives. Make sure that careful consideration is given to every potential promotional tool that will help the company make positive contacts with consumers.

Section 5.0

To begin this section, start by stating your consumer objectives and give a brief overview of plans to achieve these objectives. This includes a short description of the methodologies to be utilized. Also, note if you expect these methods to change over time. It will help to think about and identify any market trends that might have an impact on achieving the company's consumer objectives.

5.0 IMC Objective One (Consumer)

The objective for the home office segment is to create awareness of Willamette's superior quality craftsmanship, elegance, technology integration, and the ergonomically comfortable design of the company's computer furniture and to show how this furniture can maximize the utilization of the available office space. To accomplish this objective, a combination of advertising, consumer promotions, direct marketing via mail and the Web site, and a sponsorship program will be used. This market has not been tapped heavily by our competition and has not been approached through a direct marketing format. Other companies assume that these individuals buy their furniture at retail outlets. We believe

> that with the integrated approach we have designed, it will be possible to better reach this target market.

Section 5.1 Budget

As part of the budget planning process, you will need to estimate the cost of reaching all desired consumers. This includes considering every method that will help the company reach the right target markets. Once the total budget has been created, the next step is to allocate money to each of the IMC programs. The amount each element receives depends on factors such as the size and location of each target market, the consumer objectives that are being sought, the competition, and the industry. Typical IMC components to include in the budget are:

- Advertising
- Consumer Promotions
- Sponsorship
- Public Relations
- Personal Selling
- Database Programs
- Agency fees

The next step is to arrange a calendar or schedule for the advertising program. Three basic approaches can be used:

- Spend more during peak seasons to capture a higher market share and prevent erosion of your market share by competitors.
- Spend more during the slow seasons to stimulate sales and create a more uniform sales pattern throughout the year.
- Spend a uniform amount throughout the year.

When a company advertises during *peak seasons,* such as Christmas, the marketing team is placing an emphasis sending messages at the times customers are most inclined to buy. Since consumers are on the "hot spot," this approach makes sense for some products. Weight Watchers, Diet Centers, and others advertise heavily during the first two weeks of January. Many New Year's resolutions include going on a diet.

Advertising and using other promotions during peak seasons can be accomplished in two ways. The first is called a *pulsating schedule.* This schedule includes continuous communications all year with bursts of higher intensity at certain times. During peak seasons the company will schedule more advertisements in more media.

A second approach is called a *flighting schedule*. This schedule sets up marketing communications to be presented only during peak times and not at all during off-seasons. The method is best suited to seasonal products such as snow skis and swimsuits.

Advertising more during *slow sales seasons* is designed to "drum up business" when people do not regularly buy. In retail sales, slow seasons occur during January and February. Some companies advertise during these months to sell merchandise that is left over from the Christmas season.

Many marketing experts believe it is best to advertise in *level amounts*, particularly when a product purchase is essentially a "random" event. This approach is called a *continuous campaign schedule*. Many durable goods, such as washing machines and refrigerators, are purchased on an "as needed" basis. A family ordinarily only buys a new washing machine when the old one finally quits. Consequently, level advertising increases the odds that the buyer will remember a given name (Maytag, Whirlpool, or General Electric) at the right time. Also, there is a better chance that consumers will be exposed to ads close to when they are ready to make purchases.

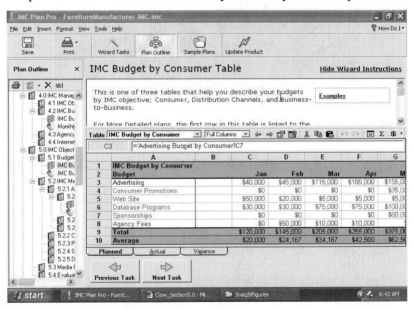

Figure 5.1 — In this table, budget figures for all of the various methods of communicating to consumers are placed, except for the advertising budget. The advertising budget is derived from another table you will complete later.

In each schedule, the goal should be to match the pacing of marketing communications with the message, media, and the nature of the product. Some media make it easier to advertise for longer periods of time. For instance, billboards are normally posted for a month or a year. They can be rotated throughout a town or city to present a continuing message about the company or its products. Some IMC components such sponsorships have to coincide with the event being sponsored, such as a rodeo, beauty pageant, or health screening clinic.

Based on a promotions opportunity analysis, estimated market growth, and IMC objectives, company leaders are able to decide how much of a budget increase or decrease is needed over the next few years. This analysis includes thinking about the promotions mix and how to use each element.

To develop your monthly IMC budget, begin by looking at the strategies, methods, and tactics you created to reach the company's consumer objectives. With the IMC plan in mind, complete the IMC consumer budget for the first year, allocating funds for each month of the year. You can modify all of the row labels to fit your IMC Plan for objective one, except for advertising. This label is fixed because the data for this row will come from the advertising budget you complete in Section 5.2.1. Here is the consumer budget for Willamette.

5.1 Budget

As the table below indicates, our budget for Objective 1 is $2,350,000. The largest portion of the budget, 41.8% or $940,000, will be spent on advertising. We believe advertising is an effective means of creating awareness among members of the home office market segment.

The second major thrust of the consumer IMC objective will be the development of a Web site and a database program to support the Web site. The primary goal of both the advertising campaign and the database program is to drive consumers to the Web site. Therefore, the budget for developing and maintaining the site will be $400,000 and the budget for developing the database program will be $465,000. We are planning three sponsorship activities during the year. These will cost approximately $260,000. Also, consumer promotions are estimated to cost $65,000.

Web site development will be undertaken in January and February. The estimated cost is $200,000. The database program will begin in February and continue through March, at an estimated cost of $150,000. By delaying the development of the database program for one month, the Web site will be initially developed, allowing the database program to be designed around the look and contents of the website.

IMC Budget by Consumer Budget	2001	2002	2003	2004	2005
Advertising	$940,000	$973,000	$1,005,000	$1,047,000	$1,090,000
Consumer Promotions	$65,000	$70,000	$70,000	$60,000	$50,000
Web Site	$400,000	$250,000	$250,000	$260,000	$270,000
Database Programs	$465,000	$500,000	$600,000	$700,000	$800,000
Sponsorships	$260,000	$260,000	$300,000	$325,000	$350,000
Agency Fees	$120,000	$130,000	$140,000	$150,000	$160,000
Total	$2,250,000	$2,183,000	$2,365,000	$2,542,000	$2,720,000
Average	$375,000	$363,833	$394,167	$423,667	$453,333

Table 5.1 – IMC Budget by consumer

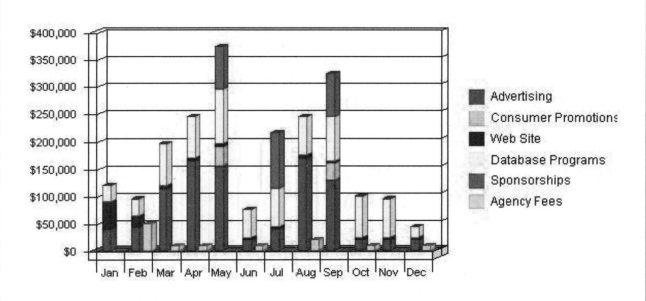

Figure 5.2 – Bar chart of IMC Budget by Consumer Monthly

Section 5.2 IMC Methodologies

This is a summary section for the consumer IMC approach. It should include a brief presentation regarding how to integrate the advertising, consumer promotions, personal selling, sponsorship programs, database programs, and any other programs to be used. In writing this section, think about how you will reach consumers and accomplish the IMC objective stated in Section 5.0.

5.2 IMC Methodologies

Reaching the consumer market (home offices) requires a blended approach. While advertising is a critical component of our IMC approach, it will be supplemented with consumer promotions, direct marketing, and a sponsorship program.

The primary role of advertising is to create awareness of our brand merchandise as well as the brand name. The consumer promotions are geared primarily to encourage trial usage. The direct marketing program is aimed at encouraging individuals to our website and to encourage trial usage. The sponsorship program's role is to create brand awareness at events that this market may be likely to attend.

Section 5.2.1 Advertising

Many people think of advertising as the most exciting form of promotion. It is important to remember, however, that advertising is just one component of integrated marketing communications. The role it plays varies by company, product, and the marketing goals that have been set. The key to advertising effectively is to see it as one of the spokes in the "wheel" of the promotional effort with the other "spokes" being the other components of the IMC approach.

For some products and companies, advertising is the central focus, with the other components (trade promotions, consumer promotions, and personal selling) used to support the campaign. In other situations, advertising may be used to support a national sales force and trade promotions programs.

In the business-to-business sector, advertising often supports other promotional activities such as trade shows and personal sales calls. In the consumer sector, the reverse is often true. Advertising is often the primary communication vehicle in reaching consumers. Other promotional tools (contests, sampling, and premiums) are then used to support the advertising function. In general, the primary goals of advertising are to:

- build brand image
- inform
- persuade
- support other marketing efforts
- encourage action

One of the most important functions of advertising is to *build a brand and/or corporate image*. This, in turn, generates brand equity. Brand equity means that a brand is the most desirable to consumers and businesses. Brand equity takes two forms: (1) a "top of mind" brand, or (2) the consumer's "top choice." When consumers are asked to identify brands which quickly come to mind from a product category, particular brands are nearly always mentioned. Those named have the property of being a *top of mind brand*. For example, when asked to identify fast food restaurants, McDonald's almost always heads the list. The same is true for Kodak film and Campbell's Soups. This is true not only in the United States, but in many other countries as well. A *top choice* brand is the first or second pick when a consumer reviews purchase alternatives.

Part of building brand image and brand equity is developing brand awareness. Advertising is the best method to reach that goal. Brand awareness means the consumers recognize and remember a particular brand or company name when they consider purchasing options. Brand awareness, brand image, brand equity are vital for success.

A second role that advertising can play is to *provide information* to consumers. The information directed at consumers includes a retailer's store hours, business location, or sometimes more detailed product specifications. Information can be offered to make the purchasing process appear to be convenient and relatively simple, which may help to entice customers to finalize the purchasing decision and travel to the store.

Another common goal of advertising is *persuasion*. Ads are often designed to convince consumers that a particular brand is superior to other brands. Some of these ads show consumers the negative consequences of failing to use a particular brand. This creates the sense that the company's product is a better alternative that helps the consumer avoid negative events. Changing consumer attitudes and persuading them to consider a new purchasing choice is normally a challenging task.

Sometimes advertising is used to *support other marketing functions.* Manufacturers employ advertising to support trade and consumer promotions, such as theme packaging or combination offers. Contests, such as the McDonald's Monopoly promotion, require extensive advertising to be effective. Retailers also utilize advertising to support marketing programs. Any type of special sale (white sale, buy-one-get-one-free, pre-Christmas sale) needs vigorous advertising to attract customers.

A final advertising goal can be to *encourage action.* Television commercials can encourage viewers to take action by dialing a toll free number. This leads to a quick purchase. Everything from Veg-A-Matics to CDs and DVDs are sold using action tactics. More recently, infomercials and Home Shopping Network programs heavily rely on immediate consumer purchasing responses.

In this section of the IMC plan, discuss the role of advertising will play in achieving your consumer objectives. Here is Willamette's advertising statement.

5.2.1 Advertising

The objective of our IMC Plan for the home office market is to create awareness. This makes advertising crucial. Frequency and reach are important. While the number of outlets used for advertising is limited, the frequency is vital. The goal is to establish the Willamette brand name in the consumer's evoked set. We recognize that office furniture is not purchased on a frequent basis. Therefore, it is critical to maintain a consistent level of advertising that ensures an ad will be seen when the consumer is in the market for office furniture or thinking about office furniture.

A secondary goal of the advertising campaign is to direct consumers to the Web site. This will help them learn more about the Willamette brand and what it offers. Our Web address will be a component of every advertisement.

A third of our advertising budget will be spent on television ads. To maximize the effectiveness of this budget, television advertising will be shown in March, April, May, August and September only. This should create the greatest impact on our customers.

Internet advertising will be placed on business-related business sites. Since this is a relatively new advertising approach for us, it will be important to evaluate each site selected in terms of hits and click-throughs.

Magazine ads will be placed in the Home Office Computing Journal. These will run all year with heavier emphasis during the months TV ads are running. We also plan during this first year to conduct a survey of our new customers to see what magazines or journals are read with the idea that next year we will move our advertising to magazines that may be a better target for our home office customers.

Section 5.2.1.1 Advertising Budget

Developing an advertising budget means deciding on media choices. Media planning begins with a careful analysis of the media habits of the target market. One method for addressing the issue of media planning is to approach it from the customer's viewpoint. The idea is to plot the choices in media that a specific, defined target market might experience through the course of a typical day. For example, this list may include the following:

- Favorite radio stations the people in a target market listen to as they travel to and from work.
- Favorite morning or evening news programs, newspapers, or Internet sites that are used to see the day's news.
- Trade or business journals used at work.
- Favorite or often-used websites at work.
- Favorite magazines the target market consumers read for leisure.
- Favorite television shows watched by people in the target market during leisure time.
- Shopping, dining, and entertainment venues

Specific details of this type are valuable as you develop a media strategy. Demographics such as age, gender, income, and education are not enough to determine the media habits of a person in a target market. Discovering viewing patterns of customers means messages can be designed to appeal to key consumers and that they will be available at the times and locations where key consumers are likely to receive messages.

Figure 5.3 — The budget figures that are placed here for advertising are totaled and will automatically become part the budget table in Section 5.1 and also in Section 4.2.

Typical media choices include television, radio, magazines, newspapers, the Internet, billboards, and direct mail. Selecting the proper blend of these media outlets is a crucial activity. In addition to understanding the unique strengths and weaknesses of each, it is also important to know how your target market relates to each. Remember that by using more than one medium you increase the chances that people in the target market will both see a message and remember it. Being exposed to ads in two different media is normally more effective than seeing two ads within the same media. For example, watching an ad on television and reading the same ad copy in a magazine is better than seeing the same television ad twice.

As you prepare the advertising media budget, think about the other components of your consumer IMC plan. Make sure the advertising budget, especially in terms of the monthly amounts, matches the other components. For example, if you are sponsoring a big event in May, you will probably need to conduct additional advertising in May or in the preceding months to enhance the sponsorship activity. The advertising budget for Willamette furniture is shown next.

5.2.1.1 Advertising Budget

Consumer advertising will be 41.8% of the $2.35 million budget for Objective One. Of the $940,000 allocated for consumer advertising, $310,000 will be for television advertising, $270,000 for Internet advertising, and $270,000 for magazine advertising. We estimate agency fees to be $90,000.

Advertising Budget by Consumer Budget	2001	2002	2003	2004	2005
Television Advertising	$310,000	$315,000	$320,000	$325,000	$330,000
Internet Advertising	$270,000	$285,000	$300,000	$325,000	$350,000
Magazine Advertising	$270,000	$280,000	$290,000	$300,000	$310,000
Agency Fees	$90,000	$93,000	$95,000	$97,000	$100,000
Total	$940,000	$973,000	$1,005,000	$1,047,000	$1,090,000
Average	$235,000	$243,250	$251,250	$261,750	$272,500

Table 5.2 — Advertising Media Budget by Consumer

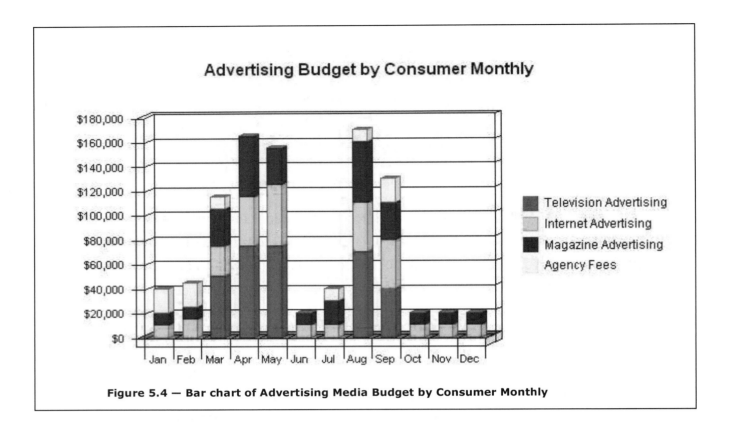

Figure 5.4 — Bar chart of Advertising Media Budget by Consumer Monthly

Section 5.2.1.2 Creative Brief

In preparing advertisements, the marketing team works from a document called a creative strategy or creative brief. The creative brief is normally prepared by the account executive. It is designed to provide key information to the creative. The creative is the person who will prepare the actual advertisement. The ultimate goal is to produce an advertisement that conveys the desired message in a manner and have a positive impact on potential customers. Here are the components of a creative brief:

- The objective
- The target audience
- The message theme
- The support
- The constraints

The first step in preparing the creative strategy is to identify *the objective* of the advertisement. The objective is the primary outcome the advertisement will try to achieve. Some possible objectives include:

- Increase brand awareness
- Build brand image
- Increase customer traffic
- Increase retailer or wholesaler orders
- Increase inquiries from end-users and channel members
- Provide information

The creative should be aware of the main objective before an advertisement can be produced. The primary objective guides the design of the advertisement and the choice of an executional theme. An ad that is supposed to increase brand awareness will have the name of the product displayed more prominently. An ad designed to build brand image may have the actual product more prominently displayed.

Next, the creative brief identifies *the target audience*. The more detail that is provided about the target audience, the easier it is for a creative to design an effective advertisement General target market profiles are not very helpful. Rather than simply specifying males, ages 20-35; more specific information is needed (e.g., males, 20-35, college educated, and professionals). Other information such as hobbies, interests, opinions, and lifestyles makes targeting an advertisement even more precise. For example, knowing the target market is females who are young, enjoy playing sports, and live an active life style provides information that is extremely beneficial in creating an appealing advertisement.

The third component of a creative brief is the *message theme*. It should spell out the specific message the IMC program intends to convey. Typical message themes focus on benefits or promises made by the company. The benefit or promise is also known as the *unique selling point.*

Message themes can be oriented toward either a rational or an emotional process. A "left-brained" ad is oriented toward logical, rational side of the brain, which manages information such as numbers, letters, words, and concepts. Left-brained advertising is logical and factual. Its appeals are rational. For example, there are logical features which are part of the decision to buy a car (size, price, special features).

At the same time, many cars are purchased for emotional reasons. The right side of the brain deals with the emotions. It works with abstract ideas, images, and feelings. A car may be chosen for its color, sportiness, or other less rational reasons. The unique selling point can be luxury or an unusual feature, such as an on-board DVD player in a mini-van.

The fourth element of the creative strategy is *the support*. Support takes the form of facts that substantiate the message theme. A pain reliever advertising claim of being effective for arthritis needs support. The point may be made by noting independent medical findings or testimonials from patients with arthritis. An ad by Pearle Vision has support that states the MicroTHINS contact lens being advertised are 30% thinner, 40% lighter, 4 times more scratch resistant, 10 times more impact resistant, 99.9% UV protection and anti-reflective than the competition. Support information should be provided to the creative prior to when the individual designs an ad.

Figure 5.5 — The creative brief will be used later to develop your actual advertisement.

The final step in the development of a creative strategy is *identification of constraints.* Constraints include the legal and mandatory restrictions placed on advertisements, as well as legal protections of trademarks, logos, and copy registrations. Constraints also include disclaimers about warranties, offers, and claims. For warranties, a disclaimer specifies the conditions under which they will be honored. For example, tire warranties often state they apply under normal driving conditions with routine maintenance. A person cannot ignore tire balancing and rotation and expect to get free new tires when the old ones wear out quickly. Disclaimer warranties notify consumers of potential hazards associated with products. For instance, tobacco advertisements must contain a statement from the Surgeon General about the dangers of smoking and chewing tobacco. Disclaimers about offers spell out the terms of financing agreements, as well as when bonuses or discounts apply. Claims identify the exact nature of the statement made in the advertisement. For example, when nutritional claims are made, there must be a statement about the size of serving or other information which makes it clear how many nutrients actually are present in the product.

A complete creative brief spells out the product's (1) key benefit, (2) type of value, (3) and the leverage point that should be used in the advertisement. To identify the key benefit, start by thinking about the product's unique selling point. Then, develop a linkage between that point and the benefit it offers to the consumer.

One method advertisers use to link a unique selling point to a *key consumer benefit* is called a means-ends chain. This approach to creating an advertisement identifies a chain made up of means that leads consumers from the product's best attribute to a feeling about desired benefit, or the desired end-state the consumer will experience.

The purpose of the means-end chain is to cause a chain reaction. Viewing the ad leads the consumer to believe that the product offers more than a benefit. It will help the consumer achieve *a personal value* such as comfortable life, excitement, freedom, happiness, inner peace, personal accomplishment, pleasure, security, self-respect, self-fulfillment, social acceptance, and wisdom.

Think about the last time you saw one of the many milk advertisements showing a celebrity wearing a white mustache. With milk, the product attribute of calcium provides the consumer benefits of being strong and healthy. The personal value that the consumer derives from healthy bones is feeling wise for using the product.

The last item in the creative brief is a note about the *leverage point* to be used. A leverage point is the feature of an ad that leads the viewer to transform the advertising message into a personal value. To construct a quality leverage point, the creative must be able to build a pathway which connects a product benefit with the potential buyer's value system. Creatives spend considerable amounts of time designing ads with powerful leverage points. The leverage point in milk advertisement is the white mustache.

Using the information above, you should be able to prepare a creative brief to serve as a guide in the development of the advertisement. Once the brief is completed, then finish this section by providing information on the means-end chain that will be used by the creative to design the ad. Here is the creative brief used by Willamette Furniture.

5.2.1.2 Creative Brief

In developing the initial print advertisement for the home office market, the following creative brief will be used.

Objective: To develop brand awareness.

Target Audience Profile: The home office market segment consists of individuals between the ages of 25 and 65. These customers typically earn incomes in excess of $100,000. Space is a major consideration for these individuals, who work out of their homes. Many of the businesses are computer-related. Consequently, the individual is a high user of computing technology. Configuration of equipment is important. Often the customer runs a one-person-business operation. Therefore, workmanship, ease of use, and ergonomics are key issues in the selection process. Even for home offices that are not business related, space and configuration are primary features.

Message Theme: The primary theme will still be that Willamette Furniture is for home office owners who want elegance, fine workmanship, integrated technology, ergonomic comfort, and practicality in their office furniture.

The Support: Willamette Furniture is recognized by business executives, home business individuals, and small business owners as a high-quality brand.

The Constraints: Made of 100% wood cannot be used in the advertisement because some small component parts are made from fiberwood. Although the furniture is 95% to 98% wood, Willamette Furniture does not want to risk and potential legal action or investigation by the FTC.

In creating the advertisement for Willamette Furniture, the following means-end chain was developed:

Unique Selling Point: Comfortable, elegant, ergonomic designed furniture.

Product Benefit: Comfortable, practical, and looks good.

Personal Values: Wisdom and comfort.

Leverage Point: Will be the headline "For the Best" which will tie the visual element to the copy in the advertisement. This will be a play on words. The concept behind the leverage point will be that Willamette offers "the best" quality furniture for the elite or "best" Home office person.

Section 5.2.1.3 Advertising Design

Advertising design is the time when the actual ad is being prepared. The advertising design process involves three decisions: (1) the creative message strategy, (2) the appeal, and (3) the executional framework. Each of these activities requires careful consideration by the advertising team.

Creative Message Strategy

The creative message strategy is the primary tactic which will be used to deliver the message theme. There are three broad categories of message strategies: (1) cognitive strategies, (2) affective strategies, and (3) conative strategies. The three represent the components of attitude.

A **cognitive message strategy** takes the form of rational arguments or pieces of information presented to consumers. The advertisement's key message focuses on the product's attributes or the benefits customers will obtain from using the product. The product's attributes can include a huge range of benefits. Foods may be described as healthful, pleasant-tasting, low-calorie, and so forth. A tool may be shown as durable, convenient, or handy to use. There are five major forms of cognitive strategies:

- Generic
- Preemptive
- Unique selling proposition
- Hyperbole
- Comparative

103

Generic messages are direct promotions of product's attributes or benefits without any claim of superiority. This type of strategy works best for a firm that is clearly the brand leader and dominant in the industry within which it operates. The goal of the generic message is to make the brand synonymous with the product category. Thus, Campbell's Soups can declare "soup is good food" without any claim to superiority because the company's products so strongly dominate the industry. Typically, when consumers think of soup, they think of Campbell's.

Preemptive messages are claims of superiority based on a specific attribute or benefit of a product. Once made, the claim normally preempts the competition from making such a statement. For example, Crest toothpaste is so well-known as "the cavity fighter" that the brand has preempted other companies from making similar claims, even though all toothpastes fight cavities. Thus, when using a preemptive strategy, the key is to be first company to state the advantage, thereby preempting the competition from saying it.

A *unique selling proposition* is an explicit, testable claim of uniqueness or superiority which can be supported or substantiated in some manner. Brand parity makes a unique selling proposition more difficult to establish. Reebok claims it is the only shoe that has the DMX technology, which provides for a better fit for their shoes. Because of patents, Reebok can claim this unique selling proposition.

The *hyperbole* approach makes an un-testable claim based upon some attribute or benefit. When NBC claims that its Thursday night line-up is "America's favorite night of television," the claim is a hyperbole.

The final cognitive message strategy is the *comparative* approach. When an advertiser directly or indirectly compares a good or service to the competition, it is the comparative method. The competitor may or may not be mentioned by name in the advertisement. Sometimes, an advertiser simply presents a "make-believe" competitor, giving it a name like product X.

Affective message strategies invoke feelings and emotions and match them with the product, service, or company. These ads enhance the likability of the product, recall of the appeal, or comprehension of the advertisement. Affective strategies elicit emotions which then in turn affect the consumer's reasoning process, and finally lead to action. An emotion such as love may help convince a consumer that a safer but more expensive car is worth the money. Affective strategies fall into two categories: (1) resonance, and (2) emotional.

Resonance advertising connects a product with a consumer's experiences in order to develop stronger ties between the product and the consumer. For example, using music from the 1960s is designed to take baby boomers back to that time and the pleasant experiences they had growing up. Any strongly held memory or emotional attachment is a candidate to be used in resonance advertising.

Emotional advertising elicits emotions that eventually lead to product recall and choice. Many emotions can be connected to products, including trust, reliability, friendship, happiness, security, glamour, luxury, serenity, pleasure, romance, and passion.

Conative strategies lead more directly to a consumer response or behavior. Conative strategies are also used to support other promotional efforts, such as coupon redemption programs, Internet "hits" and orders, and in-store offers such as buy one-get-one-free. The goal of a conative advertisement is to elicit behavior.

Action-inducing conative approaches create situations in which cognitive knowledge of the product and/or affective liking of the product may come later (after the actual purchase) or during usage of the product. For instance, a point-of-purchase display is designed (sometimes through advertising tie-ins) to cause people to make impulse buys. The goal is to make the sale, with affective feelings and cognitive knowledge forming later, as the product is being used.

Promotional support conative advertisements supplement other promotional efforts. Besides coupons and phone-in promotions, a company may advertise a sweepstakes that a consumer may enter by filling out the form on the advertisement or by going to a particular retailer.

Types of Appeals

Individual advertisements feature one key type of appeal. Effective message strategies must be carefully matched with the appeal and the executional framework. Typical appeals that have proven successful include:

- Fear
- Humor
- Sex
- Music
- Rationality
- Emotions
- Scarcity

Each of these appeals fits specific situations.

Fear appeals persuade the viewer through using some kind of frightening situation or circumstance. Life insurance companies can discuss the dangers of what happens when to a family when the parents do not have life insurance Deodorant brands can highlight the negative consequences of bad body odor.

A second type of appeal is based on *humor*. Funny messages attract attention. Often the most remembered ads use a humor appeal. The trick to humor is making sure people remember the product as well as the punch line.

Sex is routinely used to appeal to consumers. Sex appeals take the form of nude or partially nude models in an ad, sexual suggestive situations, overt or clearly sexual connotations, subliminal techniques that hint at sex, or sensuality. Sensuality promotes the product using love between two people through intimate, sensuous contact.

Many ads feature *music* in the background. Some appeals make music the major part of the ad's appeal. Well-known songs are used for this purpose.

Rational appeals are tied closely to cognitive message strategies. A rational ad appeals to an individual's rational thinking process. The goal is to present sound arguments for a product and support it with solid facts. Emotional appeals, on the other hand, attempt to appeal to an individual's feelings.

The final type of appeal, *scarcity*, promotes the idea the product is scarce and action needs to be take immediately. Scarcity is a form of conative advertising.

The appeal chosen should be based on a review of the creative brief, the objective of the advertisement, and the means-end chain to be conveyed. The actual choice depends on a number of factors, including the product being sold, the personal preferences of the advertising creative and the account executive, as well as the wishes of the client.

Figure 5.6 — In Section 5.2.1.3 you will provide additional information needed to design your ad, such as the personal value, leverage point, and desired execution.

Executional Frameworks

The manner in which an ad appeal is presented is called the executional framework. Think of an executional framework like this: The advertising appeal is like a movie script (e.g., comedy, drama, action film). The ad appeal is designed to spell out the overriding format to be used. So, if the appeal is the script, then the plot or format for the movie is the executional framework. The various styles which can be used as executional frameworks include:

- Animation
- Slice-of-life
- Dramatization
- Testimonial
- Authoritative
- Demonstration
- Fantasy
- Informative

Animation is the use of cartoon or drawn character to present the advertising message. Still animations are displayed on packages (the Jolly Green Giant). New technologies allow animations to be much more sophisticated, even to the point of blending drawn figures into real life situations.

A *slice-of-life* execution mimics a real life event. Slice-of-life executions require four steps: encounter, problem, interaction, and solution. The steps work like this: First, a television ad shows parents cheering a girl at a soccer game (encounter). Her uniform is gets so dirty that the parents fear is it will not come clean for the championship game (problem). Another parent or a voice-over then highlights the attributes and benefits of a particular brand of laundry detergent (interaction). The ad ends with the girl in a clean uniform at the championship game (solution).

A *dramatization* execution is the same as the slice-of-life, only more severe. Dramatizations rely on strong emotions, such as fear. A dramatization may show how someone survived a heart attack or car accident by using a product.

A *testimonial* execution means someone will testify about a product's benefits. The person can be a real life endorser or a celebrity. The secret is to make sure the endorser is trustworthy.

The *authoritative* approach is similar to a testimonial execution, but involves an authority presenting the benefits. The endorsement comes from an expert, such as a physician. People must believe the person has special knowledge for this execution to be successful.

A *demonstration* execution is normally shown in TV ads. It involves an actual demonstration of the product's usage. Showing a furniture polish adding luster to wood is a demonstration. To work, the viewer must be able to clearly see the improvement or a benefit.

The *fantasy execution* involves an unrealistic presentation. Fantasies can take the form of anything from a dream vacation spot to a juicy hamburger. The goal is to attach excitement and other pleasant emotions to the product or service.

The final method is called an *informative execution*. It involves presenting information to the audience in a straight-forward manner. Cognitive and rational arguments are the most compatible with an informative execution.

Almost any execution can be used within the format of one of the various appeals and creative message strategies. For example, a slice-of-life execution can depict a fear appeal and use an emotional message strategy. An informative execution can be humorous and involve an emotional or brand appeal, but so can animations. Testimonials or demonstrations may be rational or emotional, and so forth. The key is to match all of these elements in such a way that they create an effective advertisement.

Design your advertisement to match your objectives. Your goal is to create an ad that people like and one that accomplishes your IMC objective. Even if you are hiring an agency to produce the advertisement for you, you may still want to understand the design process. In this section, discuss the creative message strategy, the appeal, and the executional framework that will be used. Here is Willamette's plan of attack.

5.2.1.3 Advertising Design

In developing the print ads, Willamette will utilize the **generic** message strategy. The idea is to convey the message the Willamette brand is the "best" and is designed for the "best" consumers. This will be conveyed through an **emotional appeal.** The ad features a background that mimics the oval office of the President of the United States. The goal is to create positive emotions and even patriotic emotions. The execution that will be used will be **testimonial**. While the background mimics the oval office of the White House, the individuals in the ad will be an actual salesperson of Willamette with one of their customers.

> Our television commercials will use a slightly different approach. The creative message strategy used will be emotional, the appeal will also be emotional, and the execution will be **informative**. The ad will show how Willamette clears forests and builds their furniture, but then will move into showing how Willamette is a good corporate citizen by replanting the trees and then by being involved with Habitat for Humanity. The ad will feature an actual Habitat for Humanity project with actual Willamette employees.

Section 5.2.2 Consumer Promotions

There are many ways to entice a consumer to take the final step and make a purchase. Advertising creates interest and excitement and can be used to make consumers aware of your products. Then, many times a company uses other tactics to encourage action. Consumer promotions (sometimes called *sales promotions*) are incentives aimed at a firm's end-users or customers. The most common consumer promotions are:

- Coupons
- Premiums
- Contests and sweepstakes
- Refunds and rebates
- Sampling
- Bonus-packs
- Price-offs

A *coupon* is a form of price reduction offered to a consumer. Some coupons are distributed in free-standing inserts (FSI) in newspapers. They can be placed on a package so consumers can redeem them immediately. Other coupons are found inside of the package. This encourages repurchases since the coupon can only be used once the original product is purchased and opened. Some coupons are issued at the checkout counter, especially in grocery stores. These coupons are usually from a competing brand. For instance, when a customer buys a Duncan Hines cake mix, the machine at the cash register will produce a coupon for a Betty Crocker cake mix. Another coupon can be placed on a complementary product. For example, coupons for soft drinks can be attached to bags of potato chips.

Premiums are offers of prizes, gifts, or other special deals as part of a purchase. Premiums can be placed inside the package, such as with cereal, or as a separate item. For instance, with the purchase of a set of golf clubs the consumer may receive a free box of golf balls.

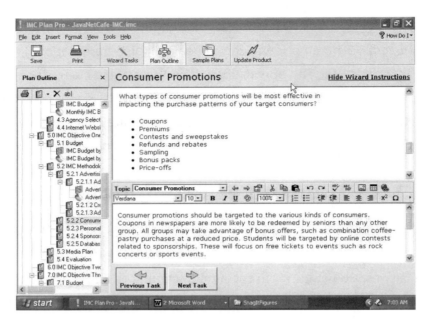

Figure 5.7 — The IMC Plan Pro software provides a list of possible consumer promotions in the instruction component of Section 5.2.2.

Contests and sweepstakes are promotions that are designed to create excitement about a product, especially a new product introduction. Contests normally require the participant to complete an activity, such as picking the four final teams in the NCAA basketball tournament. A sweepstakes, on the other hand, does not require a purchase or an activity. Participants can enter as many times as they desire. The key to both contests and sweepstakes is offering prizes that are valued or creating a game that is challenging, interesting, or fun.

A *refund* is a cash return on soft goods while a rebate is a cash return for hard goods. Both require the customer to send to the manufacturer a proof of purchase. The advantage of refunds and rebates is that manufacturers know that the discount is given to the customer.

Sampling is a method that makes it possible for consumers to try a product at no cost. It is an excellent strategy for foods, drinks, and other low-priced items. Samples are often tied in with other promotions, such as coupons. The strategy encourages consumers to try something and then make the first purchase.

Bonus packs offer additional free products with a purchase. When two cans of Pringles attached together or four bars of soap wrapped together, it is a bonus pack offer. Bonus packs allow current customers to stock on a product. This serves as a reward for customer loyalty.

A price-off is a reduction in the price of a product. The price-off can be physically marked on the product or placed there by the retailer. The purpose of a price-off is to persuade customers to try a product.

Consumer promotions incentives are aimed at getting end users to make purchases. The promotions should support the brand image and the brand positioning strategy. To ensure this occurs, it is important to understand the target audience of the program. It is also helpful to look at the competition and the consumer promotions competitors offer. Remember, consumers have choices. Use consumer promotions to enhance the odds that your brand will be selected. Willamette's approach is shown next.

5.2.2 Consumer Promotions

The budget for consumer promotions is only $65,000. Consumer promotions are not a prominent part of our IMC plan, because our market is the high-end office furniture segment. These promotions would tend to project a different image than what has been outlined in this IMC plan. Offering price reductions and coupons to consumers seeking high-end, elegant furniture is not a logical approach.

Willamette Furniture will utilize two consumer promotions. First, a deluxe golf bag with purchases will be given as a premium during the months of May and September. The golf bag, as with our furniture, will be the top of the line. It should have a strong appeal to the members of home office market.

The second consumer promotion will be a leather, top-of-the-line, personal briefcase with the owner's name embossed in gold. Again, this type of gift fits well with the personality of a member of this target market. Used in this way, premiums provide rewards for purchases. A premium is one way of saying "thank you." Neither of these premiums would motivate a person in this target market to make a purchase. Both do make a nice "thank you" present and serve as a constant reminder of who we are. They may also lead to word-of-mouth communications when one of our customer's acquaintances asks about the golf bag or briefcase.

Section 5.2.3   Personal Selling

Personal selling is sometimes called the "last three feet" of the marketing function. It represents the distance between the salesperson and the customer on the retail sales floor as well as the distance across the desk from the sales representative to the business customer. Personal contact between the sales representative and the consumer can be used to add the final touch to a successful marketing communications program.

Sales to consumers often are finalized by retail salespeople. Therefore, manufacturers and wholesalers should consider how to work with retailers. The goal is to ensure that retail salespeople have all the information they need to properly sell products. To make contact, some producers use the services of a merchandising company. Others send salespeople to visit retailers along with product information.

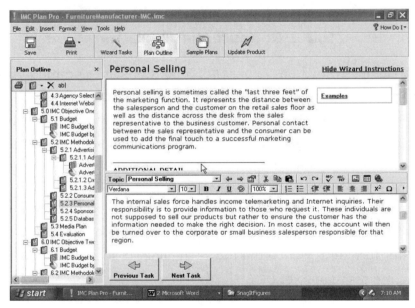

Figure 5.8 — In this section is information about the personal selling approach that will be used by Willamette Furniture.

Retailers have more options than manufacturers and wholesalers in terms of developing bonds with customers. Retail clerks interact directly with customers. To create a strong personal selling program, some questions to ask include:

- What knowledge, background, or experience is critical for your salespeople as a foundation for developing quality customer service?
- What incentives will be put into place to encourage good customer service?
- What incentives would you offer to encourage selling?

- How will we support our personal selling (e.g. point of sale brochures, Internet, advertising, etc.)?

The answers will help the company create the proper sales program. Willamette's personal selling strategy is as follows.

5.2.3 Personal Selling

The sales staff for Willamette is divided into five broad areas: corporate accounts, small business accounts, home office accounts, channel accounts, and internal sales. The home office accounts salespeople will be responsible for Objective 1 with assistance from the internal sales department.

The internal sales force handles in-bound telemarketing and Internet inquiries. These salespeople have the responsibility of providing information to those who request it. Based on an evaluation of the dollar value of the sale, the internal sales person will either handle the sale over the telephone or refer it to the home office account sale staff. If the sale is estimated at less than $1,000, the internal sales staff should handle the account. Sales estimates over $1,000 should be given to home office account salespeople. In most cases, we anticipate the sales will be handled by internal sales.

To encourage each member of the sales team to provide a high level of service, we will use a combination compensation package consisting of a salary, commissions, and bonuses. Approximately 70% of each salesperson's income should be from the salary component. They can then add to their base salary with commissions paid on each account. This will be a percentage of the gross margin to discourage our salespeople from offering customers price reductions or discounts. Bonuses are paid to all salespeople within a division for making their yearly sales quota, monthly new accounts quota, and year-end market share quota. By using both individual and group incentives, we believe our salespeople will be more dedicated to the company and helping each other achieve sales

> targets. What we don't want are high-pressure salespeople. This would be contrary to our IMC philosophy of providing our customers with information so they can make the decision to purchase from us. This same approach must be used with our entire sales staff.

Section 5.2.4.   Sponsorship Programs

Sponsorship marketing means that the company pays money to sponsor someone or some group that is participating in an activity. A firm can sponsor a practically unending list of groups and individuals. For years, local firms sponsored everything from little league baseball and soccer teams to adult bowling teams. Other organizations sponsor college scholarship programs, participate in special "days" (such as a Labor Day festivals), as well as individuals who enter various contests. Many local car race tracks feature drivers who are sponsored by various companies. On a national scale, Nike purchases sponsor "exemptions" for golf tournaments. In Tiger Woods' first year on the PGA tour, this meant he could enter a professional tournament without being "qualified" (a top money winner or winner of a tournament in the previous year). Boxers, players, and occasions (a "home run giveaway" at a baseball game) can be sponsored by a company.

Sponsorships are used to accomplish many different objectives for organizations. For example, sponsorships can:

- Enhance a company's image
- Increase the firm's visibility
- Differentiate a company from its competitors
- Showcase specific goods and services
- Help the firm develop closer relationships with current and prospective customers

In selecting a sponsorship program, the key is to match the audience profile with the company's target market. Thus, a firm will sponsor a participant at an event attended primarily by females if a company's main market is female. Marketing executives also consider the image of the individual participant or group and how it relates to the firm's image. For instance, a contestant in an "upscale" competition, such as a beauty contest, should be sponsored by a tuxedo or formal gown company. Sponsorships are designed to help the company present a unified message to all audiences which projects a positive corporate image. If possible, the firm should be the exclusive sponsor of the person or team. It is much easier to be remembered if the firm is the only sponsor compared to one of many sponsors.

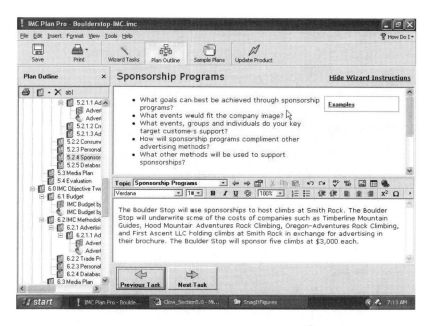

Figure 5.9 — Sponsorships are an important part of many IMC Plans because of their popularity with consumers.

Many sponsorship programs feature sporting events. Sports are popular and often attract large crowds. In addition to the audience attending the game or competition, many more watch on television. Athletes tend to be idolized by fans and can be effective spokespersons for various products. The same is true for music concerts. Several companies sponsor bands at rock and country music concerts as a means of reaching loyal listeners and fans. The idea is to take the loyalty associated with the musical entertainer and transfer part of it to the product or company serving as the sponsor of the concert.

Some organizations have moved away from sports sponsorships toward more cultural events, such as classical music groups and jazz bands, visual art exhibits by noted painters, dance troupes, and actors for various theater performances. Cultural sponsorships are not a good match for every firm. They are effective for those products which are sold to the more affluent members of society. Consequently, financial institutions are the primary sponsors of these types of performers. In the past, many institutions provided funds without receiving much recognition. Now these philanthropic efforts are being leveraged by having the name of the company strongly associated with the cultural activity. This includes printing the name of the firm on programs and regularly mentioning the brand or corporate name as being responsible for arranging for the artist to be present at the cultural event. Also, sponsors usually receive choice seats at performances which can be given to key clients.

In choosing a sponsorship program, it is helpful to think about questions such as:

- What goals can best be achieved through sponsorship programs?
- What sponsorship programs will help obtain consumer objectives?
- What events would fit the company image?
- What events, groups and individuals do the company's key target customers support?
- How will sponsorship programs compliment advertising?
- What other IMC methods will be used to maximize the impact of the sponsorship?

The Willamette sponsorship program shown below is designed to appeal to customers with more refined tastes.

5.2.4 Sponsorship Programs

Willamette plans to sponsor home and garden shows in select cities in the United States in May and again in September. In May, Willamette will be one of the sponsors for the Dallas Home Show and Atlanta Home Show. The cost will be $25,000 each. The third May show is a Home and Garden Show in Chicago, which will cost $30,000. The last series of shows will be in September. These are home shows that are smaller and cost between $10,000 and $15,000 each. These shows are held in Kansas City, San Diego, Phoenix, Nashville, Jacksonville, Charlotte, Cleveland, Cincinnati, and Detroit.

The goals of each of these trade shows are to create awareness for the Willamette brand and to prospect for leads for the consumer market. It is also possible that small business owners and even executives may attend these shows. While the attendees will be important, just as important to Willamette will be the other booth operators and owners. Many of these will be home office owners, small business owners, and business executives.

In July, Willamette will sponsor five Habitat for Humanity projects by donating $20,000 to each project and by encouraging employees to participate in the actual building projects. Employees will be allowed to work on company time.

Section 5.2.5   Database Programs

Developing an IMC database is not the same thing as database marketing. The role of the database in an IMC program is to support the total marketing effort. It is not just another marketing program, like advertising or personal selling, that just happens to use a database.

Database management is a powerful tool. It can help the marketing department reach key IMC goals. Customers often are willing to communicate important information that can be used to enhance brand loyalty, increase sales, and develop long-term relationships. Data mining ensures that your company knows the profile of its main customers. These current customers can be targeted in future promotions, and potential new customers may be discovered, especially when they have similar characteristics to those who currently make purchases. The steps in developing a database include:

- Determine the objectives of the database
- Collect data
- Build your data warehouse
- Mine data for information
- Develop marketing programs from the data
- Evaluate the marketing programs and data warehouse

Typical database *objectives* include providing useful information about a firm's customers, creating information about why customers purchase, and tracking changes in purchasing behaviors and purchasing criteria used by customers.

The second step is to *collect data.* As the marketing team gathers this information, it is important to consider the following:

- What type of information should be collected?
- How will the information be stored?
- Who will manage that process and who will have access to the information within the company?
- What information about the purchasing trends of your customers will most help your marketing efforts?

To *build a data warehouse,* it helps to understand the various ways the organization might use data. Some of the more common uses are:

- Targeting customers for a direct-marketing program such as direct mail.
- Developing a system so that field salespeople have access to important customer information as they prepare to make sales calls.
- Making it possible for internal salespeople to be able to access the database when a customer calls to place an order.
- Giving the service department and customer relations department access to customer data as they deal with inquiries and complaints

The next item is *data mining*. Mining data involves tabulating information in ways that will assist the marketing team in reaching target markets and potential new customers. Data should also be stored in such a way that it can be used in future programs. For instance, data should be set up so that a marketing program featuring in-bound phone calls reaches customers who have called to make purchases in the past.

The fifth part of database management is to set up *marketing programs* that are based on the data. Three of most common are (1) direct marketing, (2) permission marketing, and (3) frequency programs.

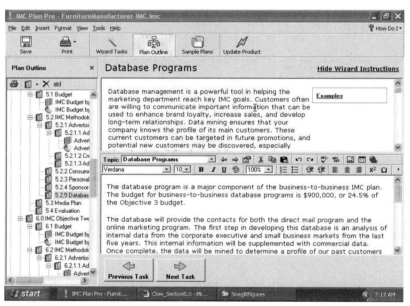

Figure 5.10 — Database marketing is an integral part of many IMC plans because of its ability to gather data and reach consumers one-on-one.

Direct marketing programs create bonds with customers by offering them the opportunity to buy directly. They enhance loyalty to a brand or company instead to the retailer. Direct marketing programs often generate greater profits, since other channel members are bypassed. Typical forms of direct marketing include the mail, e-mail, catalogs, the mass media, and the Internet. Regardless of the type chosen, it is important to display a toll-free number and a website frequently so that consumers are able to contact the company for additional information and to place an order.

Permission marketing involves sending product information and promotional information only to customers that give you permission to do so. People who are not interested do not receive your marketing materials. Return rates on permission marketing are often much higher than traditional direct marketing campaigns, since the group that is receiving your solicitations are more likely to be interested in purchasing your good or service if they have given you permission to contact them about it. In addition, customers who participate in permission programs often look forward to hearing from the company. The messages sent are normally personally relevant to the customer.

Frequency programs are incentive plans designed to encourage repeat purchase behavior. Companies develop frequency programs for two primary reasons. The first is to develop loyalty among their own customers. The second is to match or preempt the competition. Marketing experts have known for years that it is cheaper to retain customers than to try to win new ones. Seeking to keep a customer can help increase sales over time while creating a stronger bond with the individual. This bond makes it possible for the company to cross-sell other goods and services.

Building a frequency or loyalty program involves three principles. First, design a program that enhances the value of your product. Second, calculate the full cost of the program. Most frequency programs are more expensive to operate than companies estimate. In addition to the cost of the incentives, firms must allow for database costs, record keeping, mailings, and redemption of incentives. Third, design a frequency program that maximizes a customer's motivation to make the next purchase. The goal is to keep the individual from switching to another firm. Providing the proper incentives requires an understanding of your target customers.

The final part of database management is *evaluation*. This element is described in Section 5.4. Remember that database management should reach several goals, including better sales and profits as well as brand and customer loyalty. The Willamette database program for consumers is shown next.

5.2.5 Database Programs

The database program is an important component of the consumer IMC plan. The budget for consumer database program is $465,000, or 20.7% of the Objective 1 budget.

The database will provide the contacts for both the direct mail program and the online marketing program. The first step in developing this database is an analysis of internal data from the home office markets from the last five years. This internal information will be supplemented with commercial data. Once complete, the data will be mined to determine a profile of our past customers for the home office markets. With this information, we will be able to determine the best characteristics for purchasing potential mailing lists. Once our database is completed, every new transaction and every new contact will be added. This will allow us to modify our customer profile over time.

A second major use of the database will be to determine the buying potential of inquiries. Information gathered from internal information and commercial sources will be used to compare the profile of the company making the inquiry to our best customers. Such comparative power of the database will help in determining which prospects should be pursued by our internal sales staff and which should be transferred to our field salespeople.

A major component of this database program is the direct mail catalog. By profiling typical customers, our design team along with experts from our agency, Hodgsons/Meyers will be able to design a catalog that will speak to our customers. Having a name and address is not enough. We must know who they are and how to reach each decision maker. Also, we need information about their likes and dislikes. Armed with this information from our database, we can provide information to members of our target market in such a way that they can make an intelligent, informed decision. Even in the catalog, our approach will not be to sell, but to provide information. With this theme, customers will feel we are truly wanting to help them make good decisions.

Section 5.3 Media Plan

A media plan is based on the advertising budget. As the budget was created, various media where chosen. Now, more specific information and plans should be provided. This includes stating which television shows or programs will be utilized. Also, the plan spells out the actual magazines, newspapers, billboards, and other media that will feature advertisements.

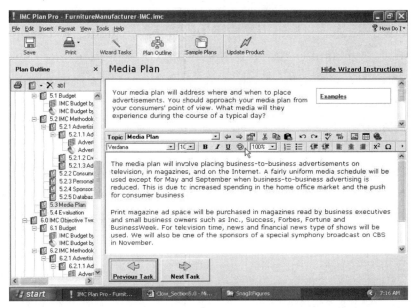

Figure 5.11 — In this section of the IMC Plan is information about the various media, such as television and magazines, which will be used to reach your consumer market.

The goal of the media plan is to match your target market with the audience characteristics of the various mediums available to you. If your target market is males, ages 40-60, then you will want to locate magazines and television programs that include this demographic group in the audience profile. While a perfect match is unlikely, you will want to maximize effective reach and effective frequency. *Effective reach* is the number of individuals within an audience market that match the target profile. *Effective frequency* refers to the number of exposures that are needed to accomplish a consumer marketing objective. Willamette's approach focuses on consumer awareness.

5.3 Media Plan

Our primary objective is to create awareness. To do so, frequency will be important. The goal is to establish the Willamette brand name in the consumers evoked set through short, repetitive advertisements. Office furniture is not purchased on a frequent basis. Therefore, it is important for consumers to have the Willamette brand in their evoked set or see an advertisement just as they are contemplating a purchase.

The television advertising will be shown in March, April, May, August and September. The primary venue will be CNN business-related television shows, such as CNN Money. We will also utilize the other news networks such as Fox News Channel and MSNews. We believe that these types of programs are watched by our target audience and will provide the image we want to convey.

Business-related sites will be used for our Internet advertising, with emphasis on news-related sites. The high cost of these ads combined with our limited budget means we will need to rotate these ads on a regular basis.

Magazine ads will be placed in the Home Office Computing Journal. These will run all year with heavier emphasis during the months TV ads are running. We also plan during this first year to conduct a survey of our new customers to see what magazines or journals are read with the idea that next year we will move our advertising to magazines that may be a better target for our home office customers.

Section 5.4 Evaluation

Section 3.7 provides an in-depth discussion of the evaluation process. In this section, you should discuss the evaluations that relate only to the consumer IMC objective. You may also choose to delete this section and provide greater detail in Section 3.7 or refer the reader to Section 3.7 for more information. Here is the brief evaluation statement for Willamette.

5.4 Evaluation

Evaluations of our consumer objective will be conducted internally and by Media Solutions. The evaluation will involve brand awareness, image analysis, positioning analysis, consumer promotions analysis, direct marketing analysis, and advertising impact

Brand awareness, image analysis, advertising impact, and the positioning analysis will provide excellent feedback concerning our consumer advertising program. Our consumer promotions program will be evaluated in May and June by Media Solutions. The Direct Marketing Analysis will provide feedback concerning our database program.

Section 6
IMC Objective Two: Distribution Channel

This section of the IMC Plan is where the marketing communications strategies associated with moving the physical product from the producer to the consumer are outlined. Your company's IMC distribution objective is going to depend on where the firm is in the distribution channel. The "traditional" channel is:

    Producer -- Wholesaler -- Retailer -- Consumer

    For business-to-business marketing, the channel can take several forms, including:

    Producer -- Industrial Agent -- Business Customer

    Producer -- Industrial Merchant -- Business Customer

A merchant is any company that takes title to goods and then resells them. An agent is a company that represents goods without actually owning them.

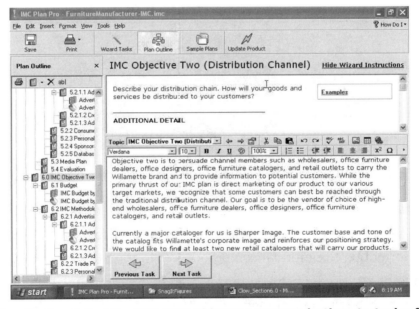

Figure 6.1 — Section 6.0 of the IMC Plan addresses communication strategies for the distribution channel.

Producers or manufacturers have different goals and use different strategies than do middlemen, such as wholesalers, retailers, agents, and merchants. A manufacturer is most interested in having company products visibly represented by firms that are in contact with consumers. Middlemen are more focused on obtaining the best possible products to represent and having a variety of goods to entice buyers.

As a manufacturer, the IMC distribution objective is probably going to be focused more on "pushing" products through the channel. Retailers want to "pull" customers into the store.

This section follows the same pattern as Section 5 on the IMC Plan Pro disk, except you are dealing with channel members instead of consumers. This means, for example, that instead of consumer promotions, the focus is on trade promotions.

Section 6.0

Section 6.0 addresses the distribution or supply chain management aspect of the IMC plan. Keep in mind that unless customers have easy access to a product, they probably will not buy it. To learn more about the distribution function, you may want to re-read the Section 3.4 discussion of distribution strategies.

Start section 6.0 with a brief overview of this entire section. Remember to highlight the objectives for the distribution channel. Here is Willamette's distribution channel statement.

6.0 IMC Objective Two (Distribution Channel)

Objective two is to persuade channel members such as wholesalers, office furniture dealers, office designers, office furniture catalogers, and retail outlets to carry the Willamette brand and to provide information to potential customers. While the primary thrust of our IMC plan is direct marketing of our product to key target markets, we recognize that some customers can best be reached through the traditional distribution channel. The goal is to be the vendor of choice of high-end wholesalers, office furniture dealers, office designers, office furniture catalogers, and retail outlets.

Currently, Sharper Image is a major cataloger for Willamette products. The customer base and tone of the catalog fits Willamette's corporate image and reinforces our positioning strategy. We would like to find at least two new retail catalogers to carry our products.

A primary distribution channel will be custom office furniture contractors. These companies are more effective at reaching the corporate executive because they custom design offices and provide office furniture to fit accordingly. Two such businesses, Rocky Mountain Desk Corporation and Quasius Contract Furniture already work closely with us to incorporate our furniture into their office designs.

Another important channel will be high-end office dealers such as Curtis Furniture and Wilson Office Furniture. Both businesses operate dealerships that match our target market and corporate image. In the selection of dealers, we would like to offer dealers an exclusive advantage that would assure them that we will not have any direct competitors with our line of products.

Section 6.1 Budget

Typically distribution channels programs are not as visible as those used to attract consumers. It is easy to under-budget or underestimate the importance of IMC distribution objectives. Keep in mind, however, that in most industries approximately 50% of all marketing dollars are spent on developing the distribution channel. Retailers spend less, because they often receive funds and support from trade promotions offered by manufacturers and middlemen. Your IMC distribution budget should match the type of company, product, and your distribution objectives.

You can refer to Section 5.1 for information about budgeting. The main role of the trade promotions and the channel communications is to push the product through the channels. The marketing programs designed by the competition are probably going to force your company to use trade promotions in order to maintain good relations with channel members. The idea is to encourage them to push your products.

Figure 6.2 — For products sold in retail stores, the typical budget for trade promotions is at least 50 percent of the total IMC budget. The total distribution IMC portion of the budget would be even a higher percent.

You can obtain the overall budget for this objective from Section 4.2. The task now is to break this budget into its component parts. In most cases, this includes:

- Advertising
- Trade promotions
- Personal selling
- Database programs

Here is the breakdown for Willamette Furniture.

6.1 Budget

The budget for developing this distribution channel for the next year is $1,040,000. As shown in the following table, $300,000 has been budgeted for trade promotions. These funds will be spent primarily on wholesalers, office furniture dealers, and retail outlets that carry our products. We are budgeting $240,000 for channel advertising in office furniture and computer furniture trade journals. We are budgeting $240,000 to support our sales staff. This money is not for salaries, but for additional expenses incurred by our sales staff. It also includes contest money which will be held twice a year. We will spend $180,000 on database programs and $80,000 on agency fees, primarily for our advertising agency, Hodgsons/Meyer.

The heaviest months for disbursements of the distribution budget will be January through March and October through November. A major reason for this pattern is that we did not want heavy promotions and efforts into our distribution plan during the same months that we are concentrating in our consumer market.

IMC Budget by Distribution Channel					
Budget	2001	2002	2003	2004	2005
Advertising	$238,000	$255,000	$270,000	$285,000	$300,000
Trade Promotions	$300,000	$330,000	$340,000	$350,000	$360,000
Personal Selling	$240,000	$310,000	$320,000	$330,000	$340,000
Database Programs	$180,000	$200,000	$210,000	$220,000	$230,000
Agency Fees	$80,000	$85,000	$90,000	$95,000	$100,000
Total	$1,038,000	$1,180,000	$1,230,000	$1,280,000	$1,330,000
Average	$207,600	$236,000	$246,000	$256,000	$266,000

Table 6.1 – IMC Budget by Distribution Channel

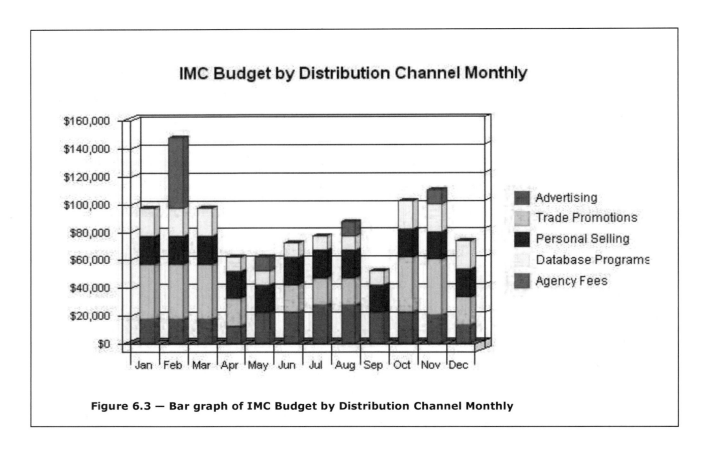

Figure 6.3 — Bar graph of IMC Budget by Distribution Channel Monthly

Section 6.2 IMC Methodologies

It is important to integrate your distribution strategies with consumer strategies. Therefore, this section is where to restate your consumer IMC approach. Give a brief overview of how you will integrate advertising, trade promotions, personal selling, database programs, and any other programs with distribution. In writing this section, think about how the product will move through the channel. State how you intend to accomplish the IMC objective presented in Section 6.0. Here is Willamette's IMC methodology statement.

6.2 IMC Methodologies

Personal selling will be the major promotion tool used to increase our distribution channel and to develop strong relationships with those who become partners with us. Trade promotions, which the salespeople will have authority to disburse, will help us gain an advantage over our competitors. Co-op advertising programs are especially important in the development of this channel.

To supplement the trade promotions and selling efforts, we will advertise in trade journals and on the websites of channel members. The latter will be important for attracting retailers to stock our merchandise and for office designers who may be looking on the Internet for information about office furniture they can incorporate into their office designs.

Section 6.2.1   Advertising

Advertising to members of the distribution channel is different than advertising to consumers. A manufacturer or wholesaler working to persuade major distributors to carry its product will focus less on the benefits of the product and more on other information. A manufacturer with a strong brand name has a major advantage. Still, even major manufacturers use advertising to encourage channel members to stock and push their products. Refer to Section 5.2.1 for more information about advertising. Here is Willamette's approach to advertising to members of the channel.

6.2.1 Advertising

Advertising for Objective 2 will be limited to trade magazines and the Internet. Messages will be targeted to middlemen to encourage them to stock Willamette's products. The advertisements will vary depending on which channel member is being targeted in the advertisement.

Trade journals in which we will purchase advertising space are Furniture Trade Journal and Furniture Design and Manufacturing Journal. Both are used by dealers, retailers and other members of the marketing channel. To supplement the trade journals, ads will be purchased on Internet directories such as FDM Online and Furniture.web.

Section 6.2.1.1   Advertising Budget

To establish an advertising budget that matches the distribution program, the first issue is to make quality media choices. Media planning begins with a careful analysis of the media habits of the target audience, which, in this case, consists of channel members. One method for addressing the issue of media planning is to approach it from the customer's viewpoint. The idea is to plot the choices in media that a specific, defined target market might experience through the course of a typical day.

Trade journals are the most frequently chosen medium for distribution channels. Almost every industry has at least one or more trade journals that are used by members within that industry. Other media that can be used include television, radio, magazines, newspapers, the Internet, billboards, and direct mail.

For more information about developing the advertising media budget, please see Section 5.2.1.1. In this section, Willamette chose trade journals and the Internet to reach channel members.

6.2.1.1 Advertising Media Budget

Of the $240,000 allocated to channel advertising, $155,000 will go to trade journals and $60,000 will be used for the Internet, with the remaining $25,000 agency fees to Hodgsons/Meyers.

Advertising Budget by Distribution Channel

Budget	2001	2002	2003	2004	2005
Trade Magazines	$155,000	$190,000	$200,000	$210,000	$220,000
Internet	$60,000	$65,000	$70,000	$75,000	$80,000
Agency Fees	$25,000	$0	$0	$0	$0
Total	$240,000	$255,000	$270,000	$285,000	$300,000
Average	$80,000	$85,000	$90,000	$95,000	$100,000

Table 6.2 — Advertising Budget by Distribution Channel

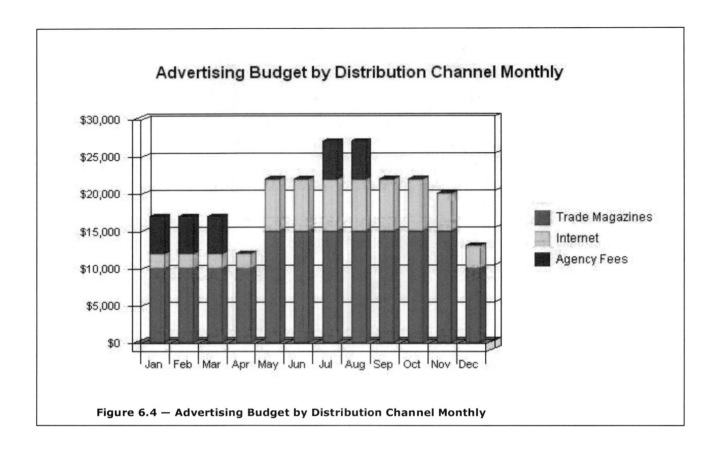

Figure 6.4 — Advertising Budget by Distribution Channel Monthly

Section 6.2.1.2 Creative Brief

Section 5 introduced creative briefs. You will need to prepare one for the advertising program that focuses on distribution channels. The objectives and methods for distribution may be different than those set for consumers.

To complete this section, prepare a creative brief using the guidelines given in Section 5.2.1.2. Be sure to include the means-end chain. Instead of consumer value, you will identify a distribution channel value. The Willamette Furniture distribution channel creative brief is next.

6.2.1.2 Creative Brief

In developing the initial print advertisement for the Furniture Design and Manufacturing Journal, the following creative brief will be used.

Objective: To generate inquiries into stocking Willamette furniture or adding Willamette furniture to their product portfolio.

Target Audience Profile: The targets of these advertisements are office furniture wholesalers, furniture dealers, office designers, office furniture catalogers, and office furniture retail outlets. All these businesses are concerned with profit margins and sales. They want to know how adding the Willamette line will benefit their business.

Message Theme: The primary theme is that Willamette Furniture fits individuals and businesses who want elegance, fine workmanship, integrated technology, ergonomic comfort, and practicality in their office furniture. For the distribution market, the theme is carried one step further to include the distributor as an important link to that customer.

The Support: Willamette Furniture is recognized by business executives, home businesses individuals, and small business owners. Willamette's reputation and intensive IMC program will help sell the furniture for the distributor.

The Constraints: Willamette wants only the best distributors, therefore exclusive rights accompany all agreements.

In creating the advertisement for Willamette Furniture, the following means-end chain was developed:

Unique Selling Point: Elegant, ergonomically designed furniture.

Benefit: The furniture sells itself to the distributor's target market.

Distribution Channel Value: Less selling effort required.

Leverage Point: Will be the headline "For the Best" which ties the visual element to the copy in the advertisement. The concept behind the leverage point will be that Willamette offers the best quality furniture for "select" distributors and to be selected by Willamette means we think you are among the best.

Section 6.2.1.3 Advertising Design

When the creative brief is complete, the next step is advertising design. Think about what message strategy will communicate effectively with your distributors. What type of appeal should be used and what type of executional framework will be the most effective? Remember, the motives for channel members are to stock brands that will sell. Marketing to channel members is different than to end users. Channel members are primarily interested in how your product will create sales, boost profits, and enhance business.

Refer to Section 5.2.1.3 for information about the content of advertising design. Use it as a guide for 6.2.1.3. Here is the design statement for Willamette.

6.2.1.3 Advertising Design

Print ads for the distribution channel will follow the consumer print advertising imagery to ensure consistency of message. The same brand image message strategy will be used. The idea is to convey the message the Willamette brand is the "best" and is designed for the "best" distributors. This will be conveyed through a **rational appeal**, instead of an emotional appeal. Willamette offers an exclusive distributorship to only select distributors, which will add prestige to the product line. The executional framework that will be used will be **testimonial**. While the background mimics the oval office of the White House, the

> individuals in the ad will be an actual salesperson of Willamette with one of his customers. Copy will indicate that with Willamette furniture, the distributor will boost their sales.
>
> The Internet ads will be similar but will contain fewer words and a smaller picture.

Section 6.2.2   Trade Promotions

One of the most expensive and important parts of a distribution program is the trade promotions that are offered. Trade promotions are the expenditures or incentives used by manufacturers and other members of the marketing channel to help push products through to retailers. These incentives are designed to entice channel member to purchase goods for resale. Trade promotions are aimed at retailers, distributors, wholesalers, brokers, or agents. Wholesalers, distributors, brokers, and agents can also use trade promotions. The goal is to entice retailers to purchase products for eventual resale.

The difference between trade promotions and consumer or sales promotions is that the latter involves a sale to an end-user or customer. When a manufacturer sells products to another business for end use, the enticements involved are consumer or sales promotions tools. On the other hand, when a manufacturer sells to another business for the purpose of having the good resold then it is a trade promotion.

Effective trade promotions are an integral part of an IMC program. Unfortunately, in some companies, the individual handling trade promotions is not involved in the IMC planning process. Trade promotions are viewed as being merely a means for getting products onto retail shelves or satisfying some channel member's request. To satisfy the demand by administration to increase sales, trade managers often feel greater and greater pressure to use trade promotions to push their products. Little consideration is given to the other components of the IMC program when trade promotions programs are developed.

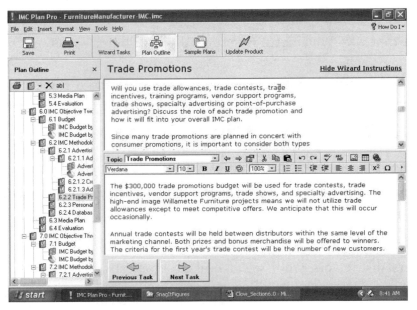

Figure 6.5 — Trade promotions are a critical component of the IMC Plan since it ensures your product will be on store shelves so customers can make a purchase.

To solve this problem, the marketing executive must incorporate trade promotions into the overall IMC approach. Tie-ins between advertising campaigns and trade promotions can help companies achieve more "bang" for their marketing bucks. Since the goal is to generate tangible sales and other measurable outcomes, the account executive also has a vested interest in bringing the trade promotions program in line with the other parts of the IMC plan. Typical trade promotion objectives are:

- Obtain initial distribution
- Obtain prime retail shelf space or location
- Support established brands
- Counter competitive trade and consumer promotions
- Increase order sizes
- Build retail inventories
- Enhance channel relationships

A variety of trade promotional tools exist. These items are used by manufacturers as well as other members of the trade channel. The most common trade promotions are:

- Trade allowances
- Trade contests
- Cooperative merchandising agreement
- Training programs
- Cooperative advertising programs

- Trade shows
- Point-of-purchase displays

A *trade allowance* is one of the more common trade promotions used by manufacturers and others in the channel. The purpose of a trade allowance is to offer financial incentives to other channel members in order to motivate them to make purchases. The channel member then is in a better position to offer discounts or other deals to consumers. Trade allowances can be packaged into a variety of forms. Two of most often used are off-invoice trade allowances and slotting fees.

An *off-invoice allowance* is a price discount on an order. To receive the discount, the channel member must order a minimum amount. For instance, a manufacturer may offer a 10% off-invoice discount if a retailer orders at least 1,000 cases by a certain date.

The second type of trade allowance is a *slotting fee*. These are funds paid to retailers to carry merchandise in stock. The fee is usually a one-time charge for a new product that is being introduced. Since shelf space at retail stores is limited, adding a new product means reducing or deleting the shelf space available for other products. Therefore, retailers often charge a slotting fee to place the new product on the shelf. Slotting fees can run from a few thousand dollars to as much as one million dollars.

Another way to achieve sales targets and other objectives is by offering *trade contests*. Rewards are given as contest prizes to brokers, retail salespeople, retail stores, wholesalers, or agents. These funds are known as spiff money. The rewards can be items such as luggage, a stereo, a television, or a trip to an exotic place such as Hawaii. Contests can be held at various levels, such as brokers versus brokers, wholesalers versus wholesalers, or retail stores within a chain versus each other.

The most comprehensive trade incentive is a CMA or *Cooperative Merchandising Agreement*. A CMA is a formal agreement between the retailer and manufacturer to undertake a cooperative effort. The agreement may be about retailer advertisements that also mention the manufacturer's brand. Another approach is to feature the manufacturer's brand as a price leader. Also, a cooperative agreement can be made to emphasize the manufacturer's brand in an in-house offer made by the retail store, or a special shelf display featuring a price incentive. The advantage of the CMA agreement in featuring various price breaks is that the manufacturer knows that the price allowance is being passed on to the customer. One final form of CMA is a special in-store display that the retailer agrees to use on specific dates or for a specific time period. For example, when Coors beer features a display featuring supermodel Heidi Klum during Halloween, a special cooperative merchandising agreement may be reached with individual liquor stores in order to get them to set up the displays.

Training programs for channel members, especially retail salespeople, can help a manufacturer achieve several IMC objectives. Retailers and wholesalers often sell multiple brands. Many manufacturers are willing to provide training to wholesaler or retailer salespeople to help them learn more about the manufacturer's products. This makes it more likely that the salesperson will emphasize the manufacturer's brand instead of competitors. Having additional knowledge about one brand aims salespeople toward that brand. Also, if the salesperson feels like he or she is getting special treatment, such free lunches or other small favors as part of the training program, the salesperson will have more positive feelings about the company that gave them.

Many channel members participate in *co-op advertising*. In a co-operative advertising program, the manufacturer agrees to reimburse the retailer a certain percentage of the advertising costs associated with advertising the manufacturer's products in the retailer's ad. To receive the reimbursement, the retailer follows specific guidelines concerning the placement of the ad and its content. In almost all cases, no competing products can be advertised. In most cases, to receive the reimbursement, the manufacturer's product must be prominently displayed. There may be other restrictions on how the product is advertised as well as specific photos or copy that must be used.

Trade shows are an excellent way to bring channel members together. From a manufacturer's standpoint, a trade show offers the opportunity to discover potential customers and sell new products. Also, relationships with current customers can be strengthened at the show. A trade show often provides the chance to find out what the competition is doing. Many times, trade shows present a situation in which the manufacturer's sales team can meet directly with decision makers and buyers from business-to-business clients. A trade show can be used to strengthen the brand name of a product as well as the company's image.

From the buyer's perspective, a trade show offers a place to examine several suppliers in a short period of time. In some cases, the buyer is able to negotiate special deals. Trade shows are an ideal place for buyers and sellers to meet in an informal, low-pressure setting.

Point-of-purchase (POP) programs consist of any form of special display that features merchandise. A store shelf or point-of-purchase display represents the last chance for a manufacturer to reach consumers. POP displays may be located near cash registers in retail stores, at the end of an aisle, in a store's entryway, or any other place where they will be noticed. Point of purchase advertising includes displays, signs, structures, and devices that are used to identify, advertise, and/or merchandise an outlet, service, or product. POP displays serve as an important aid to retail selling.

POP can be used to make an impression just before a purchase is made, or to leave an impression when the buyer exits the store. POP displays are highly effective tools for increasing sales. About 50% of the money spent at mass merchandise stores and supermarkets is unplanned. The purchases are known as *impulse buys.*

The choice of which trade promotions to feature depends upon whether you are selling to a wholesaler, distributor or a retailer, company preferences. The IMC plan and your distribution objectives should guide your choices. Since many trade promotions are planned in concert with consumer promotions, consider both types of promotions simultaneously. If the company is going to offer a major consumer sweepstakes, you may want to spend more money on point-of-purchase displays for retailers to ensure customers see the sweepstakes offer. The Willamette Furniture trade promotion plan features trade contests, cooperative merchandising agreements, and trade shows.

6.2.2 Trade Promotions

The $300,000 trade promotions budget will be used for trade contests, trade incentives, vendor support programs, trade shows, and specialty advertising. The high-end image Willamette Furniture projects means we will not utilize trade allowances except to meet competitive offers. We anticipate that this will occur occasionally.

Annual **trade contests** will be held between distributors within the same level of the marketing channel. Both prizes and bonus merchandise will be offered to winners. The criteria for the first year's trade contest will be the number of new customers. This type of contest fits with our overall marketing goal of expanding the distribution channel. By using members in the channel to help us develop the channel, the work is made easier. Contest winners will be declared in October and November.

For trade incentives, **cooperative merchandising agreements** will be used. This allows the Willamette brand to be featured in advertisements targeted to the distributor's customers. While price features may be occasionally used to match any competitive offers, the goal is to develop CMAs with every distributor for advertising space and prominence. Closely connected to the trade incentives will be cooperative advertising through our vendor support program. The cooperative advertising program will reimburse channel members up to 75% of the cost of an advertisement featuring Willamette Furniture. To receive the reimbursement, Willamette must be prominently featured in the ad and no other competing office furniture manufacturer can be shown.

National **trade shows** within the office furniture industry will be an important element in recruiting channel partners. Willamette's marketing team will attend trade shows early in the year (January through March). Through the trade shows, we hope to generate prospects to contact during the year by members of our sales staff. As part of our trade show and as giveaways for our salespeople, we will give away small specialty advertising items such as calendars, pens and deskpads.

Section 6.2.3   Personal Selling

Personal selling is a vital link between vendors and clients in the distribution channel. Many marketing teams carefully invest in and study how to make quality sales presentations to potential channel members. Selling within the channel structure requires identifying viable channel customers, qualifying those prospects, and developing positive relationships. The goal is to provide a fluid chain originating with the manufacturing and ending with the final customer. Personal selling programs should answer questions such as these:

(1) Which channel members are the most likely to carry our products?

(2) How will we qualify these prospects?

(3) What qualifications or specifications should channel members meet?

Channel members that pass this initial screening are the ones to have the sales force contact.

Channel members routinely enter into contractual agreements with vendors. The idea is to ensure a continual supply of needed products. A contract guarantees that a stable price and regular delivery of the good or service.

Unfortunately, too many contractual relationships are adversarial rather than being based on mutual trust. This often leads to dissatisfaction between the parties and a change in vendors at the end of the contractual period. Consequently, many channel members find it of value to develop trusting relationships with other companies based on things besides contracts. When the buyer and seller know each other and work well together, trust can be the result.

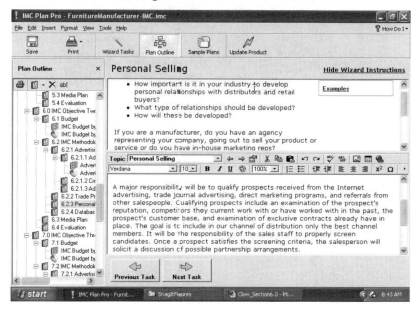

Figure 6.6 — Personal selling is an essential part of pushing products through the distribution channel.

One method that can be used to expand the level of trust between two companies is called an Electronic Data Interchange (EDI) relationship. EDI relationships occur when one company provides full access to and shares data with another business. Firms routinely exchange purchase orders, shipping notices, debit and credit memos, production rates, and other information through some EDI programs. Retail sales data obtained through the cash register scanners can also be shared with vendors. This helps the manufacturer understand what is selling and where. Sharing information involves some risk that the data will be somehow misused. EDI only takes place when the firm's leadership team fully trusts that the vendor will use information properly. Major retail operations find that EDI relationships are essential to doing business.

Keep in mind that most channel members also carry competing brands. Therefore, it is essential to think about how to establish positive relationships with channel customers to ensure your product's success. Here is Willamette's personal selling approach.

6.2.3 Personal Selling

At first we will rely solely on our sales staff to contact channel members. As business expands, we will consider utilizing manufacturing reps. Our sales staff is divided into five broad areas: corporate accounts, small business accounts, home office accounts, channel accounts, and internal sales. Salespeople in the channel accounts division will have the responsibility of dealing with the various channel members.

Our salespeople will have the responsibility of qualifying prospects. A prospective customer list will be obtained from contacts made through Internet advertising, trade journal advertising, direct marketing programs, and referrals from other salespeople. Qualifying prospects include an examination of the prospect's reputation, competitors they current work with or have worked with in the past, the prospect's customer base, and examination of exclusive contracts we already have in place. The goal is to include in our channel of distribution only the best channel members. Once a prospect satisfies the screening criteria, the salesperson will solicit a discussion of possible partnership arrangements.

In addition to developing new accounts, salespeople are responsible for servicing current accounts. It is important that salespeople develop strong relationships with each channel member. Our concern is not how many channel members we have but how strong of a relationship we have with each. The long-term goal of each partnership is to move that client toward a strategic partnership with our firm where we can work together for the benefit of both companies.

Section 6.2.4. Database Programs

Another key ingredient in a successful distribution channel program is developing a quality database. The differences between a distribution channel databases and a consumer or business-to-business databases are the functions provided. The distribution channel database generated primarily for salespeople to use before contacting channel members and servicing those accounts.

Therefore the data should help the sales force find information about channel members that is useful and helpful to selling and maintaining relationships.

Review section 5.2.5 on your IMC Plan Pro disk for information about how to build a database. Use that model for your distribution channel database program. Here is Willamette's approach.

6.2.4 Database Programs

We have a limited sales staff at Willamette. Consequently, developing an accurate data warehouse is essential. We need records about every channel member, including information about who they are, what they purchase, when they purchase and other details. These records should be readily accessible to members of our sales staff. When a sales representative is at a customer's location or with a prospect, the salesperson should have the ability to access everything we know about that client. This includes information about what type of specialty advertising the client prefers as well as topics to discuss during the sales presentation. We want the salesperson to have access to the customer's past purchase history and the trade promotions that have been used, along with information about what impact those trade promotions had on sales.

For our sales staff, the role of this database is two-fold. First, it will provide the salesperson with an accurate record of each customer. Second, it provides instant ordering and tracking capabilities to the salesperson and client. With just a few clicks of a mouse, both will be able to locate the customer's order and to discover where it is and when the merchandise will be delivered. More importantly, if that customer now needs cherry instead of oak, the change can be made on the spot as manufacturing receives the notice.

Section 6.3 Media Plan

Most media plans for distribution channels are limited to trade journals and the Internet. Almost every industry has a trade journal for members of the distribution channel. More often than not, buyers also will look at the Internet when seeking out suppliers. In selecting advertising media for your IMC program, however, it is important to go beyond trade journals and Internet sites, and to decide which other media your distribution channel members might see.

When selecting media, think about your company's advertising goals as well as its approach to distribution. Firms using an extensive distribution channel will try to encourage new channel members to carry products. This requires more extensive advertising and the use of more media than would be need for a selective or exclusive distribution strategy. Selective and exclusive distribution strategies mean that media selection is often driven by the desire to build brand equity or brand awareness. Notice that Willamette relies on the two common media for its advertising program. The company has chosen an exclusive distribution strategy, which allows for more limited channel advertising.

6.3 Media Plan

To reach our distribution channel members, continuous advertising in trade journals and on the Internet will be used. The monthly budget for trade journals and the Internet will be increased from May through November. The purpose of advertising is to generate leads for our sales staff and to generate brand awareness.

Section 6.4 Evaluation

It will help you to review Section 3.7 for an explanation of the various methods of evaluation. When determining how to evaluate the distribution component of your IMC plan, be sure the evaluation methods match the objectives you stated in Section 6.0. The objectives of your distribution program are likely to be to increase the number of orders through distribution channels and to improve communication and goodwill between the company and its channel partners.

Immediate sales are usually the short-term goal and with improved relationships as a longer-term goal.

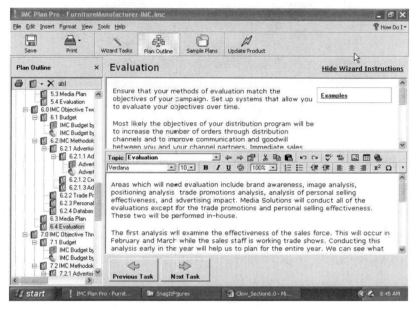

Figure 6.7 — Because of the large expenditures for the distribution channel and especially for trade promotions, developing an effective method of evaluation is important.

You can evaluate distribution channels by tracking the sales through the various channels. Longer-term objectives such as goodwill are more difficult to systematically evaluate. Some marketing teams survey channel partners to get opinions about their distribution channel efforts and the relationships they have tried to build. Willamette's evaluation includes both a sales component and analysis of the company's database program.

6.4 Evaluation

Since the sales force is major component of our distribution IMC Plan, we need to examine its effectiveness. This will occur in February and March while the sales staff is working trade shows. Conducting this analysis early in the year will help us to plan for the entire year. We can see what worked the previous year and what did not work. The trade shows also allows us ample opportunity to obtain a wide sample for the survey without the cost of telephone calls or personal interviews. We want to measure customer satisfaction as well as actual sales figures.

In April, we will examine trade promotions. We will look at the promotions we used in the past and how each impacted sales. We will study the trade promotions that we are planning, to see how they have performed in the past and what we would expect in the future. The database warehouse that was discussed in the section on Database Programs will be the key to this analysis. To avoid wasting dollars, we need a measure of how well each trade promotion has functioned in the past. At the same time, we cannot allow the past to dictate the future policies. Trade promotions that have not worked well in the past may work well in the future under new circumstances and with different channel members.

The impact of our advertising to members of the distribution channel will be evaluated in September and October. It will be completed in conjunction with a larger study conducted by Media Solutions as they examine advertising impact for all three objectives. These analyses will help us to evaluate our advertising and the message approach we are sending.

Section 7
IMC Objective Three: Business-to-Business

Business-to-business customers are often vital and lucrative outlets for goods and services. They do require a slightly different IMC approach than other customers. There are several potential new clients to examine as you develop a business-to-business promotions plan.

One potential buyer is a *manufacturer.* Selling to manufacturers requires a clear understanding of the production process and how a material is used in completing a finished item. Meeting quality standards and other stringent specifications is essential. Marketing to manufacturers also requires an understanding of the manufacturer's customers.

Many goods and services are sold to various groups within the *federal, state, or local government.* Companies selling to governmental agencies must first understand that there may be a bidding process involved. Clear specifications are spelled out by the agency regarding the characteristics of the product or service. Governmental contracts can be enticing. A host of companies may become interested when bids are taken for various goods or projects, such as a new building. Companies seeking to sell to the government must develop specialized marketing techniques and have sufficient access to information to be successful.

Another major source of revenue comes from selling to *institutional buyers.* There are many non-business and nonprofit organizations seeking goods and services. Institutional buyers include colleges and universities, hospitals, charitable organizations, churches, political parties, museums, unions, and others. These organizations require many of the same office supplies, fixtures, communication machinery (phones, faxes, and computers), office equipment, clocks, intercom systems, and other products that profit-seeking firms use. The large number of nonprofit organizations means this marketplace is inviting. Company leaders should not ignore them as target markets are identified. Many of these organizations use formal bidding processes similar to those utilized by governmental agencies.

Retailers can also be business-to-business customers for items such as major equipment, computerized cash registers, maintenance supplies, and operating supplies. Keep in mind that when these retailers are business customers they are purchasing products for consumption or use in their operations, not for re-sale. Products that are re-sold are part of the distribution channel, which was described in Section 6.0.

Finally, there are a large number of *service operations* ranging from restaurants, to plumbers, to airlines. All of these need goods and services to operate.

149

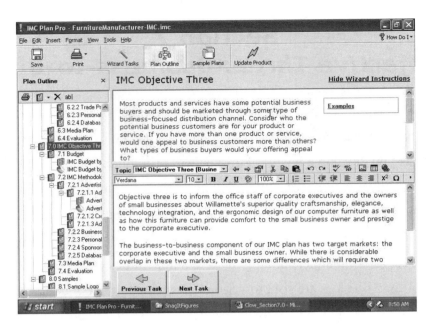

Figure 7.1 — This section of the IMC Plan addresses the communication strategies for reaching business customers.

Most goods and services have potential business buyers and should be marketed through a business-focused approach. Consider who the potential business customers are for your company. Re-read Section 3.5 for more information about the business-to-business market segment.

Section 7.0

This section of the IMC Plan is where you name the marketing communications strategies you will use to reach business buyers. It follows the same pattern as Section 5 and Section 6. There difference is that the companies you are dealing with are businesses rather than consumers or the distribution channel. Begin section 7.0 by providing a brief overview of this entire section. Be sure to highlight your communication objectives for the business-to-business market segment. Here is Willamette's overview.

7.0 IMC Objective Three (Business-to-Business)

Objective three is to inform the office staff of corporate executives and the owners of small businesses about Willamette's superior quality craftsmanship, elegance, technology integration, and the ergonomic design of our computer furniture as well as how this furniture can provide comfort to the small business owner and prestige to the corporate executive.

The business-to-business component of our IMC plan has two target markets: the corporate executive and the small business owner. While there is considerable overlap in these two markets, there are some differences which will require two separate approaches at times. For example, the primary communications to the corporate executive market will be targeted to the executive's staff since they are the ones who tend to make actual purchase decisions. The corporate executive may be the influencer of the decision, but many times is not involved at all in the actual selection and purchase decision. It could very likely fall to the administrative assistant. On the other hand, with small business owners, it is almost always the business owner who is the decider. He or she must be sold on the benefits of Willamette furniture.

Section 7.1 Budget

To set up your business-to-business budget, gather the information you prepared in section 4.2 first. Your task at this point is to break this budget down into its component parts. If you need to review information about the budgeting procedure, review Section 5.1. Typical components found in the business-to-business budget include:

- Advertising
- Business-to-business promotions
- Personal selling
- Database programs

For business-to-business promotions, keep in mind these are not trade promotions. Business-to-business promotions would be the same as consumer promotions, except they are aimed at business customers instead of retail consumers. This means you may use coupons, premiums, price-offs, bonus packs, and so forth. Review Section 5.2.2 for a discussion of consumer promotions. The budget Willamette has prepared for its promotion plan follows.

7.1 Budget

As the following table indicates, the budget for Objective 3 is $3,710,000. The largest portion, 40.4% will be used for advertising. Personal selling will be allocated $910,000 and database programs will be allocated $900,000. The smallest percentage of the budget will go for business-to-business promotions, $310,000 or 8.4% of the Objective 3 budget. Approximately $90,000 will be paid to our advertising agency for producing advertisements.

In order for the Objective 3 budget to mesh with our consumer objectives, less will be spent on business-to-business communications during May, August, and September. Our firm pushes the consumer market more heavily during those three months. This approach allows for crossover help from the business-to-business side to the consumer side of our marketing effort. It will also reduce the need to contract out or hire part-time internal sales people during May and September. Expenditures are reduced slightly in April because May is a big month for the consumer side of the business.

Many businesses make purchase decisions throughout the year. Therefore, we will always maintain a certain level of advertising and promotion aimed at this group. Also, because we have been in the business-to-business market longer than the consumer market, we need to maintain our presence in the market but we do not need to do any type of heavy promotion to build awareness.

IMC Budget by Business-to-Business

Budget	2001	2002	2003	2004	2005
Advertising	$1,500,000	$1,570,000	$1,635,000	$1,705,000	$1,765,000
Business-to-Business Promotions	$310,000	$320,000	$330,000	$340,000	$350,000
Personal Selling	$910,000	$1,050,000	$1,100,000	$1,150,000	$1,175,000
Database Programs	$900,000	$925,000	$950,000	$975,000	$1,000,000
Agency Fees	$90,000	$95,000	$100,000	$105,000	$110,000
Total	$3,710,000	$3,960,000	$4,115,000	$4,275,000	$4,400,000
Average	$742,000	$792,000	$823,000	$855,000	$880,000

Table 7.1 — IMC Budget by Business-to-Business

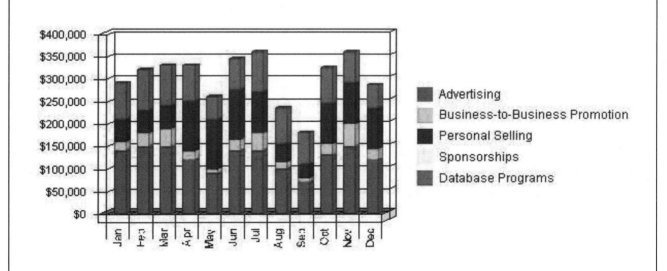

Figure 7.2 — Graph of IMC Budget by Business-to-Business Monthly

Section 7.2 IMC Methodologies

This is a summary section for the business-to-business component of your IMC Plan. Present a brief overview of how you plan to integrate advertising, business promotions, personal selling, database programs, and other programs to cultivate your business-to-business customers. The idea is to improve communication between your company and your business users and increase sales from those customers. Details regarding each tactic are described in the sections that follow. The Willamette overview notes that business-to-business customers tend to be heavy users of the Internet.

7.2 IMC Methodologies

To reach both of our target markets requires a blend of marketing communication tools. Advertising will be a central part of the plan but will be supplemented with strong personal selling and database programs. Direct marketing is a major key to success in this market. Both of our business-to-business markets are, by default, heavy users of the World Wide Web. Therefore, it is necessary to develop an aggressive Internet program.

While business promotions will be used, they are not a major emphasis in our IMC program. Our goal in this market is to provide information to the members of these target markets about our products. We believe, given correct and full information, that members of these target markets will choose Willamette Furniture. Catalogs sent by direct marketing and in response to advertising will be one method of marketing directly to the decision makers. The Internet will be the other direct marketing venue.

Section 7.2.1 Advertising

It is probably a good idea to review the material in Section 3.5 about buying centers before developing your business-to-business advertising plan. Advertising design varies based on which member of the buying center is being targeted. It may also help to review the materials in Section

5.2.1 about advertising in the consumer market. Many of the same principles apply to the business-to-business market.

In this section, discuss your advertising strategy for the business-to-business market and how it will be integrated with the other components of your b-to-b communications plan. Willamette's advertising plan is designed to support other marketing activities rather than attempting to be the primary communication platform.

7.2.1 Advertising

Advertising will be used to support the direct marketing and database programs. Advertising will encourage viewers to either access Willamette's website or call for a catalog that will provide more information. The ads are not designed to persuade viewers to buy, but to request additional information.

Advertising provides a supportive role to direct marketing and the database program. In addition to encouraging requests for more information, advertising will be responsible for developing brand awareness, creating the right image and establishing an effective position with our business customers.

Section 7.2.1.1 Advertising Budget

An advertising budget should be created as the marketing team makes media choices. Media planning begins with a careful analysis of the habits of the target market. In this case, the media habits of business-to-business customers are studied. One method used to examine these habits is by approaching them from the customer's viewpoint. The goal is to find media that buyers would use during the course of a typical day. Business-to-business buyers may listen to radio while at work. Also, it may be possible to identify the television shows they watch at home along with the Internet sites they would be most likely to visit, both at work and at home.

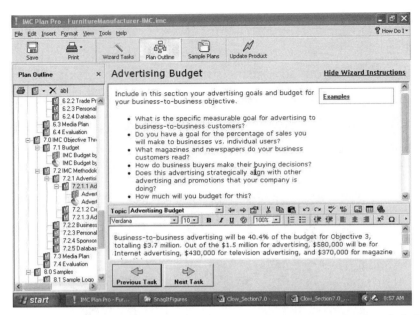

Figure 7.3 — In developing the advertising budget for the B-to-B market, it is important to think about how you can effectively reach the business buyers.

Trade journals are the most common medium used for business-to-business advertising. Almost every industry has one or more trade journals targeting members of the industry. Unfortunately, there is an increasing amount of clutter in trade journals. As a result, more businesses are switching to other media such as television, radio, magazines, newspapers, the Internet, and billboards to reach business consumers. The Super Bowl, which in the past contained only consumer ads, now features business-to-business ads. Many companies believe that business buyers may be more reachable during non-work hours than during work hours and through the traditional business-to-business media channels.

You can review Section 5.2.1.1 for more general information about developing an advertising media budget. Willamette's budget is displayed next.

7.2.1.1 Advertising Budget

Business-to-business advertising will be 40.4%, or $1.5 million, of the $3.7 million budget for Objective 3. Within the advertising budget, $580,000 will be for Internet advertising, $430,000 for television advertising, and $370,000 for magazine advertising.

Advertising Budget by Business-to-Business

Budget	2001	2002	2003	2004	2005
Magazine Advertising	$370,000	$380,000	$390,000	$400,000	$410,000
Internet Advertising	$580,000	$600,000	$625,000	$650,000	$675,000
Television Advertising	$430,000	$450,000	$470,000	$490,000	$500,000
Agency Fees	$120,000	$140,000	$150,000	$165,000	$180,000
Total	$1,500,000	$1,570,000	$1,635,000	$1,705,000	$1,765,000
Average	$375,000	$392,500	$408,750	$426,250	$441,250

Table 7.2 — Advertising Budget by Business-to-Business

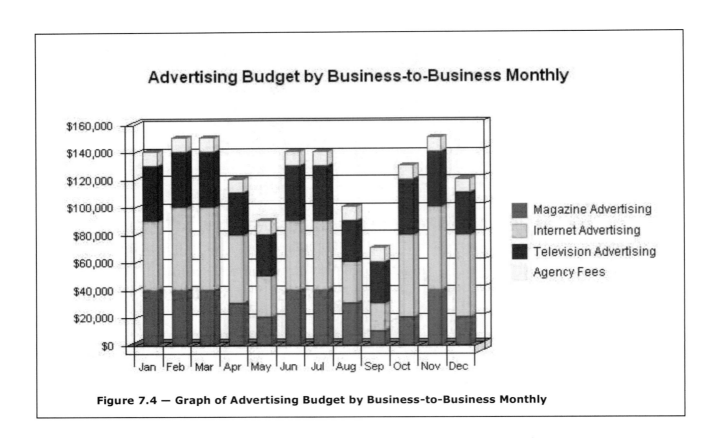

Figure 7.4 — Graph of Advertising Budget by Business-to-Business Monthly

Section 7.2.1.2 Creative Brief

Advertising to business customers is similar to advertising to consumers. The marketing team should identify specific objectives to accomplish, such as increasing brand awareness, spurring sales, or enhancing a company's image. This means you will need to prepare a creative brief for your business-to-business customers. Use the guides that were presented in Section 5.2.1.2. Be sure to include the means-end chain. Instead of consumer value, you will identify a business value. Here is Willamette's creative brief.

7.2.1.2 Creative Brief

For the small business owner market, the following creative brief will be used.

Objective: To generate inquiries for more information and to develop brand awareness.

Target Audience Profile: The small business owner tends to be between 30 and 65 years old and earns a salary of $50,000 or more annually. In most cases, the small business owner is an entrepreneur who started the business rather than by purchasing a company from someone else. The primary issue in selecting furniture is comfort. This means the small business person is normally involved in the purchase decision. The individual tends to be a medium user of computers and related equipment.

Message Theme: The primary theme will still be that Willamette Furniture is for individuals and businesses who want, elegance, fine workmanship, integrated technology, ergonomic comfort, and practicality in their office furniture.

The Support: Willamette Furniture is recognized by business executives, home business individuals, and small business owners as a high-quality brand.

The Constraints: Made of 100% wood cannot be used in the advertisement because some small component parts are made from fiberwood. Although the furniture is 95% to 98% wood, Willamette Furniture does not want to risk and potential legal action or investigation by the FTC.

In creating the advertisement for Willamette Furniture, the following means-end chain was developed:

Unique Selling Point: Comfortable, elegant, ergonomic designed furniture.

Benefit: Is comfortable, practical and looks good.

> **Business Value**: Wisdom and comfort.
>
> **Leverage Point:** Will be the headline "For the Best" which will tie the visual element to the copy in the advertisement. This will be a play on words. The concept behind the leverage point will be that Willamette offers "the best" quality furniture for the elite or "best" small business owners.

Section 7.2.1.3 Advertising Design

The creative brief should guide the next task, advertising design. As you prepare ads, think about the message strategy that will communicate effectively with business customers. Make sure the type of appeal used along with the type of executional framework all mesh to convey a strong, clear message. Advertising design is described in detail in Section 5.2.1.3. You may want to refer to that section for information about how to design your business-to-business advertising. Willamette's goal is to provide a similar, consistent message. This makes sense, since there is such a large overlap in customers in business-to-business markets and the channel of distribution.

7.2.1.3 Advertising Design

Print ads for the business-to-business will be very similar to our consumer print ads. The goal is to ensure consistency of message. The same brand image message strategy will be used. The idea is to convey the message that the Willamette brand is the "best" and is designed for the "best" business people. This will be conveyed through an emotional appeal since the ad will feature a background that mimics the oval office of the President of the United States. The ads are designed to create positive and even patriotic emotions. Most business buyers tend to make rational decisions. Still, we believe that when it comes to office furniture, an emotional appeal will be more effective, for two reasons. First, it is rarely used in business-to-business advertising, which will allow our ads to stand out. Second, we believe that in the case of the executive's staff, there is an emotional need to ensure a good quality decision is made and for the small business owner, we believe there is an emotional need to feel they have succeeded in business, thus they can afford good furniture.

The execution that will be used will be testimonial. While the background mimics the oval office of the White House, the individuals in the ad will be an actual salesperson of Willamette with one of his business customers.

Internet ads will be similar but will contain less wordage and a smaller picture.

Section 7.2.2   Business-to-Business Promotions

Sales promotions are used in the business-to-business arena just as they are for consumers. Consumer promotions were first presented in section 5.2.2. Some of the business promotions that can be used include:

- Sampling
- Price-offs
- Refunds and rebates
- Bonus packs
- Premiums
- Coupons
- Contests and sweepstakes

Product sampling is an excellent method to encourage business customers to try an item. Changing a new vendor may feel risky to a business customer. The higher the risk the person feels, the less likely he or she will be willing to try your product. Sampling is used to let the buyer try out a product without feeling any risk. By tying the sample to another promotion, such as a coupon, price-off, or bonus pack, the vendor can encourage a customer to try the product more than once.

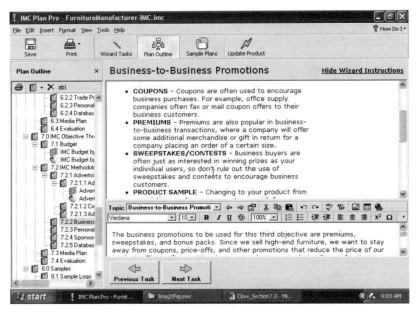

Figure 7.5 — The promotions that are used for businesses are the same as the consumer promotions, except they are directed towards a business buyer.

Price-off programs help vendor cope with competitive pressures. Price-off deals can be another affective approach to stimulating trial usage. Price-off plans work best when they are offered for products where there is little differentiation. In other words, price is the overriding factor in the purchase decision.

Refunds and rebates are promotions that are designed to encourage current customers to take action and make orders. They also can be used to counter competitive actions. With these promotions, the business customer pays full price. Refunds and rebates are not well accepted when the business buyer has to mail in proofs-of-purchase to get the money. Instead, business buyers prefer price-off deals.

Bonus packs reward current customers by giving them more for their money. They can also be used to counter competitive actions, especially since it encourages customers to stockpile a brand.

Premiums or giveaways can be used in the business-to-business sector. Care must be taken, however, because some organizations have policies against employees receiving free merchandise or gifts from salespeople or sales organizations.

Coupons are not used frequently in the b-to-b market. The reason is that a business buyer does not want to keep them until a purchase is made. Internet-delivered coupons have achieved some success in stimulating sales and trial usage, because they can be stored and/or redeemed electronically.

Contests and sweepstakes encounter the same problems as premiums. Many employees are prohibited from participating in them on the job. Consequently, they are not widely used in promoting business-to-business sales.

Be sure to coordinate your business promotions with your IMC elements as you write this section. If there is going to be a special advertising campaign in June and July, you may want to offer your current customers a bonus pack and new prospects free samples at the same time. In Willamette's business-to-business promotion plan, notice that they have found a way to incorporate a sweepstakes, by aiming it at company executives.

7.2.2 Business-to-Business Promotions

The business promotions to be used for this third objective are premiums, sweepstakes, and bonus packs. Since we sell high-end furniture, we want to stay away from coupons, price-offs, and other promotions that reduce the price of our products. The craftsmanship, elegance, and ergonomic design for our furniture combined with our high-end image means we should minimize the use of business promotions. These promotions should be non-price related.

Premiums are an important component of the business promotions. For both markets, we will offer new golf bags with purchases of office suites. Since buyers in our target market like to play golf, the golf bag should do well. For those individuals who are not golfers, we will offer a premium of season tickets for the orchestra of their choice. This premium may be more attractive to some female customers.

The **sweepstakes** is aimed primarily for the staff of corporate executives. With each corporate inquiry, up to three members of the executives staff will be entered into a sweepstake with two grand prizes of an all-expenses paid trip to Hawaii. The opportunity to win a free trip to Hawaii should be more appealing to executive staff member than would a golf bag or tickets to the orchestra.

> The final trade promotion is a **bonus pack**. During specific months of the year, July and November, we will offer bonus packs consisting of offers such items as two filing cabinets for the price of one, two printer stands for the price of one, two bookcases for the price of one, and an extra guest chair with the purchase of two. We believe these bonus packs will be especially attractive to the small business owner who wants our furniture but has a limited budget.

Section 7.2.3   Personal Selling

Personal selling is a part of many business-to-business contacts. Firms can use a variety of methods to reach b-to-b customers. These include field salespeople, inbound telemarketing, and outbound telemarketing programs.

Field salespeople identify prospects and make sales visits to the potential customer's place of business. *Outbound telemarketing* can be used to handle smaller accounts and assist in qualifying prospects as well as servicing current accounts. *Inbound telemarketing* can handle customer inquiries and either complete the sale over the phone or pass the lead onto a field sales rep.

Personal selling by field salespeople consists of five steps:

(1) identifying prospects

(2) qualifying prospects

(3) knowledge acquisition

(4) the sales call and presentation

(5) follow-up

The first step in the selling process is *identifying prospects* or potential customers. Prospects can be found through methods such as customer leads, databases, trade shows, advertising inquiries, Internet inquiries, sales promotions, and networking. The goal of prospecting is to develop a list of companies that can be approached with a personal sales call. Developing effective prospecting tactics requires careful planning.

The second step is *qualifying prospects.* This is the process of choosing companies that have the highest potential to become new customers. Sales calls are expensive. This makes the selection process a vital activity. One method of qualifying prospects is to group them into categories based on their potential. For example the "A" or best category would contain those that have the highest sales potential, "B" prospects would have less potential, "C" even less, and so forth. The idea is to decide whether or not a particular prospect is a good fit for the selling firm.

Concentrating sales efforts in specific industries can provide a firm with expertise and economies-of-scale in that industry. It also helps the company build a strong brand name and brand image in that industry.

After prospects have been qualified, the third step in the selling process is the *knowledge acquisition* stage. The goal here is to gather the information needed to make an effective sales presentation. The more specific information a salesperson has about a prospect, the greater the potential for making a sale. The information may also be used to either disqualify a prospect or upgrade the prospect to a higher category. When the knowledge acquisition step provides information suggesting the prospect is not a good fit for the company, the prospect should be either dropped from the prospect list or downgraded to a lower priority. The same would be true if a competitor is firmly entrenched with that customer. When the information indicates a company has unfulfilled needs and can be influenced by the firm's current trade promotions mix, then the prospect may be upgraded to a higher priority category.

It is a mistake to skip the knowledge acquisition stage and jump directly into making sales calls. Salespeople may make this mistake, because commissions are paid for making sales, not acquiring knowledge. It is true that too much time can be spent gathering information, however, in most cases, salespeople tend to spend too little time acquiring this critical information. Information that can be useful to a salesperson includes:

- Who the current vendor is.
- Who the prospect's customers are.
- What the prospect's current needs are.
- The role of price, service, and product attributes in the purchase decision.
- The role and importance of business promotions in the purchase decision.
- The risk factors for the prospect if they were to switch vendors.

The fourth step is the *sales call and presentation*. Sales presentations made to other businesses tend to be more complex than those made to consumers in retail situations. The first complication is that salespeople often face difficulties in getting past gatekeepers when trying to reach members of the buying center. This is a major problem when a company is in the early stages of a purchasing decision-making process and is trying to identify its needs. Only the current vendor is likely to have convenient access. This gives the current vendor the advantage of being able to cross-sell other goods and services. Consequently, the current vendor's sales team will work hard to help business customers identify needs.

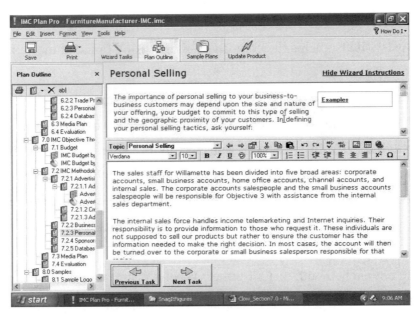

Figure 7.6 — Personal selling is an essential element of reaching business buyers.

As crucial as the initial sales presentation is to selling firms, the *follow-up* may be even more critical. This final step in the selling process should be designed to keep customers happy so that they will purchase again. Unhappy customers not only defect to a competitor but also spread negative word-of-mouth communications. It is much more cost effective to retain an old customer rather than to find new ones. Therefore, the critical role that a follow-up plays in selling program cannot be overemphasized.

Before writing this section of your IMC Plan, you may want to review Sections 5.2.3 and 6.2.3 for additional information about personal selling. Discuss how personal selling will be used to accomplish Objective 3 and how it will be integrated with your other IMC components such as advertising and business promotions. The Willamette personal selling statement is very similar to the one made for regular customers.

7.2.3 Personal Selling

The sales staff for Willamette has been divided into five broad areas: corporate accounts, small business accounts, home office accounts, channel accounts, and internal sales. The corporate accounts salespeople and the small business accounts salespeople will be responsible for Objective 3 with assistance from the internal sales department.

The internal sales force handles income telemarketing and Internet inquiries. Their responsibility is to provide information to those who request it. These individuals are not supposed to sell our products but rather to ensure the customer has the information needed to make the right decision. In most cases, the account will then be turned over to the corporate or small business salesperson responsible for that region.

To encourage each member of our sales staff to provide a high level of service, we will use a combination compensation package consisting of a salary, commissions, and bonuses. Approximately 70% of each salesperson's income should be from the salary component. They can then add to their base salaries with commissions paid on each account. This will be a percentage of the gross margin to discourage our salespeople from offering customers price reductions or discounts. Bonuses are paid to all salespeople within a division for making their yearly sales quota, monthly new accounts quota, and year-end market share quota. By using both individual and group incentives, we believe our salespeople are more dedicated to the company and will help each other achieve sales targets. What we don't want are high-pressure salespeople. This would be contrary to our IMC philosophy of providing our customers with information so they can make the decision to purchase from us. This same approach must be used with our entire sales staff.

Our field salespeople will work closely with our internal salespeople to qualify prospects. This will be obtained from information in our database, from the Internet, and from the perspective customer. Our sales staff is too small to call on every person who makes an inquiry about our products. It will be the responsibility of our internal sales staff to decide which prospects should be given to field salespeople and which should be handled via the Internet and telemarketing.

Section 7.2.4 Sponsorship Programs

Business-to-business sponsorships are the same as the consumer sponsorship. Consumer sponsorships were described in Section 5.2.4. The one difference is that the business-to-business sponsorships are aimed toward businesses rather than retail customers. Please see Section 5.2.4 for a general discussion of sponsorships.

Willamette Furniture is not planning any sponsorship programs for its business customers. So instead, The Boulder Stop sponsorship program is shown here. It illustrates how to write up the business-to-business sponsorship section. Notice that The Boulder Stop is going to sponsor rock climbs up Smith Rock in conjunction with several agencies and companies. In exchange, Boulder Stop can hand out advertising brochures. For each climb, The Boulder Stop will underwrite $3,000 of the costs. This type of sponsorship fits with its target markets and will provide an excellent opportunity to gain exposure with climbers.

7.2.4 Sponsorship Programs

The Boulder Stop will use sponsorships to host climbs at Smith Rock. The Boulder Stop will underwrite some of the costs of companies such as Timberline Mountain Guides, Hood Mountain Adventures Rock Climbing, Oregon-Adventures Rock Climbing, and First Ascent LLC holding climbs at Smith Rock in exchange for advertising in their brochure. The Boulder Stop will sponsor five climbs at $3,000 each.

Section 7.2.5 Database Programs

The business-to-business database program is same as was used to create the consumer database, as described in Section 5.2.5. It is also the same as distribution channel database program discussed in Section 6.2.4. You should re-read Section 5.2.5 for a general discussion of how to develop a database. Remember, there are three primary types of programs that originate from a database: direct marketing, permissions marketing, and frequency programs. Using this information, identify how you will develop your business-to-business data warehouse and how it will be used in your IMC Plan to communicate to your business customers. Willamette's database program focuses on direct mail, online contacts, customer inquiries, and the company's catalog.

7.2.5 Database Programs

The database program is a major component of the business-to-business IMC plan. The budget for business-to-business database programs is $900,000, or 24.5% of the Objective 3 budget.

The database will provide the contacts for both the direct mail program and the online marketing program. The first step in developing this database is an analysis of internal data from the corporate executive and small business markets from the last five years. This internal information will be supplemented with commercial data. Once complete, the data will be mined to determine a profile of our past customers for each of the two markets. With this information, we will be able to determine the best characteristics for purchasing potential mailing lists. Once our database is completed, every new transaction and every new contact will be added. This will allow us to modify our customer profile over time.

A second major use of the database will be to determine the buying potential of inquiries. Information gathered from internal information and commercial sources will be used to compare the profile of the company making the inquiry to our best customers. Such comparative power of the database will help in determining which prospects should be pursued by our internal sales staff and which should be transferred to our field salespeople.

A major component of this database program is the direct mail catalog. By profiling typical customers, our design team along with experts from our agency, Hodgsons/Meyers will be able to design a catalog that will speak to our customers. Having a name and address is not enough. We must know who they are and how to reach each decision maker. Also, we need information about their likes and dislikes. Armed with this information from our database, we can provide information to members of our target market in such a way that they can make an intelligent, informed decision. Even in the catalog, our approach will not be to sell, but to provide information. With this approach, customers will feel we truly want to help them make good decisions.

Section 7.3 Media Plan

The media plan you will prepare for this section is the same as other media plans you have constructed. Choose the media which are the best for your company, message, theme, and IMC objectives. Willamette's media plan is broken down into buys from television, magazines, and the Internet. These represent the best ways to reach business-to-business prospects and customers.

7.3 Media Plan

The media plan involves placing ads on television, in magazines and on the Internet. A fairly uniform schedule will be used except for May through September when the business-to-business advertising will be reduced due to an increase spending in our other target markets.

For our business customers, ad space will be purchased in magazines read by businesspeople, such as Inc., Success, Forbes, Fortune and BusinessWeek. For television, we will concentrate on news and financial programs on CNN and Fox. We will also be a sponsor of a special symphony broadcast in CBS in November. We feel this will reach our high end, corporate executives.

Internet advertising will be placed on a variety of business sites rather than a portal such as Yahoo. Our customers tend to be heavy users of computers. Consequently, ads featured on financial websites, news websites, and other business-oriented websites will be the most effective.

Section 7.4 Evaluation

Business-to-business promotional efforts should be evaluated to make sure they are having the proper impact. The various methods of evaluation were first explained in Section 5.3. A quick review of that information will help you prepare this section. As you determine your evaluation methods be sure they match the objective stated in Section 7.0. Willamette's program is focused on brand awareness.

7.4 Evaluation

Evaluations of business-to-business objectives will be conducted both internally and by Media Solutions. These evaluations will coincide with evaluations of Objective 1 and Objective 2. Data will be collected for the total IMC program, then separated by objective for analysis.

Brand awareness will be evaluated during June by Media Solutions. They will conduct a random survey of individuals that fit the corporate executive and the small business markets. The awareness level will be compared to previous data. If brand awareness has not increased with the current advertising approach, then it will allow us time to modify the advertising approach for the second half of the year.

In addition to brand awareness, we should make sure the information disseminated through advertising is being interpreted correctly by our business customers. Therefore, we will conduct an advertising impact analysis in September and October. Media Solutions will use attitude and recognition tests to measure feelings as well as knowledge of Willamette products. More importantly, they will analyze each of the mediums separately, television, magazines, and the Internet. This will allow us the ability to track each medium to know for future years which medium provides the most effective advertising.

The positioning analysis will be conducted October. If the position does not fit the projected position of the firm, it will allow us to modify our IMC campaign for the next calendar year.

The impact of the business promotions will be measured during May and June in connection with the analysis of consumer promotions. Based on the analysis of our consumer promotions by Media Solutions, decisions can be made about the usage of business promotions.

Customer complaints and product returns will be measured and monitored on a continual basis. We will not be able to position ourselves in this sector unless our production facility delivers on what we promise. All customer complaints or product returns will be forwarded to our marketing department for recording and analysis.

The direct marketing program will be evaluated in November and December. This will allow time to see the impact of the major mailings to both business markets. It will also give time to evaluate the effectiveness of the online direct marketing program. The direct marketing campaign is vital to our IMC campaign. Media Solutions will be charged with the responsibility of evaluating the successes of these efforts.

Section 8
Samples

Section 8.0

This is the section where you complete the final details of your IMC program. It includes preparing a sample logo, some directions for your advertisements, the forms of promotions to be used, and any other creative designs that are part of the program. In section 8.0, write a summary stating which of these will be used in your company.

Section 8.1 Sample Logo

A memorable logo can be a key ingredient in an IMC program. Some consumers are more likely to recall a visual image than a verbal message. An effective logo should pass two tests. First, consumers must remember that they have seen the logo in the past. Second, the logo should remind consumers of the brand, company, or corporate name. The logo should be attractive and match the image and theme of the rest of the marketing program.

Your IMC Plan Pro directions are to create a sample logo in the form of a graphic (*.bmp, *.gif, *.wmf, *.jpg) and insert it here using the Insert > Image command. The following logo was developed for a company called the JavaNet Internet Cafe.

Section 8.2 Sample Consumer Advertisement

In this section, your task is to prepare a sample consumer *print advertisement.* In a later section a storyboard for a television ad is prepared. There are several guidelines to use in preparing the sample consumer advertisement.

First, decide if the ad will be shown in color or in black and white. Remember that color reproduction is not as good for newspapers. Magazine advertisements in color will be more brilliant and attractive.

Second, remember that the copy for the ad should be limited. The amount of copy depends on: (1) the size of the actual ad, (2) the type of product being used, and (3) the type of executional framework. *Larger sized* ads can contain more copy than smaller ads. Advertisements for *products* that are less complicated normally require fewer words and descriptions than more complicated goods or services. A rational *executional framework* involves more copy and explanation than many of the other forms.

Third, it is crucial that you write an ad headline that captures the reader's attention. In just a few words, your headline should lead the reader to look for the promise of a benefit. If the headline fails, the rest of the ad fails.

Fourth, make sure the sample ad meshes with other components of your IMC plan, especially the current objective. It should also be appropriate for the magazine or newspaper in which it will be published.

Finally, be sure to include all vital information. This includes the company's Web site address, hours of business, location, or any other item the reader should know.

Your Advertising Plan Pro directions are to create a sample magazine or newspaper advertisement designed to reach your consumers in the form of a graphic (*.bmp, *.gif, *.wmf, *.jpg) and insert it here using the Insert > Image command. Notice the use of color, excitement, and romance in this advertisement for Cravings. Also, note that the company's Web site is featured in the ad.

Section 8.3 Sample Business-to-Business Advertisement

This advertisement is also a *print advertising* format. It should follow the same basic guidelines as the previous section. The Willamette advertisement shown below has no copy. It may represent a new trend in business-to-business advertising, one in which the appeal is more emotional (conative) than rational (cognitive).

The next step for you is to create a sample advertisement designed to reach the business-to-business audience in the form of a graphic (*.bmp, *.gif, *.wmf, *.jpg) and insert it here using the Insert > Image command. This advertisement is the one that was previously described in the business-to-business objective 3 section.

Section 8.4 Sample Storyboard

For your television advertisement, the next task is to create a sample story board. The storyboard guides the production process. Television advertisement producers should be able to look at the story board and know what they will need to shoot. For each frame on the story board, create a description of the image with verbal content to go with each picture. Both the pictures and the verbal explanation are provided for a Boulder Stop advertisement below.

Your IMC Plan Pro instructions tell you to create the sample story board in the form of a graphic (*.bmp, *.gif, *.wmf, *.jpg) and insert it here using the Insert > Image command. It will help you to review the different forms of executions (animation, slice of life, dramatization, authoritative, demonstration, fantasy, informative) before beginning work on your storyboard. Also remember that the advertisement should focus like a razor on the key IMC objective you prepared earlier.

Board #1 – Illustration of a male and female shopping in The Bolder Stop for climbing gear with the male commenting about the excellent quality of the merchandise and the female replying they also have an excellent selection. The male should be holding and looking at a rope.

Board #2 - Both the male and female climbers are in the process of climbing a rock. The female comments that this is really a tough climb. The male agrees.

Board #3 - The female arrives at the top of the rock and is looking down at the male below who is still climbing towards the top. The male looking up says I can't believe you made it first. She replies with a laugh and smile.

Board #4 - The male climber loses his grip from the rock and is suspended in mid-air. The female, in a panic voice, asks, "Are you okay?" The male replies, "Yes, the safety rope held!"

Board #5 - With the help of the female, the male climber is able to reach the top of the rock safely. As they sit at the top looking out over the valley, the female says to the male, "I'm sure glad we bought you that new rope from The Boulder Stop." The male replies, "I am too."

Board #6 - The two climbers are talking to friends in The Boulder Shop, sipping a cup of espresso coffee. The television advertisement will end with the logo flashing across the screen "Only one stop! The Boulder Stop!"

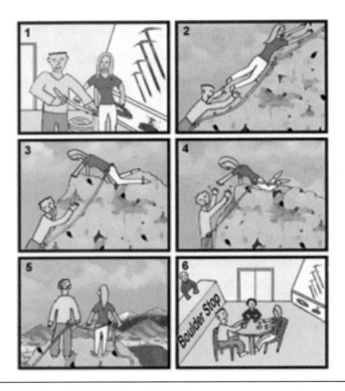

Section 8.5 Sample Web Page

The final activity in this IMC plan is setting up a sample Web page. The page should be easy to access and navigate. It should be attractive. The primary focus should be on the company's image and the IMC theme and objective you have developed. Remember that both individual consumers and business-to-business buyers may go to the site. Create links that will guide them to the proper page.

The IMC Plan Pro instructions are to create a sample Internet page for your website in the form of a graphic (*.bmp, *.gif, *.wmf, *.jpg) and insert it here using the Insert > Image command.

When you have finished this task, your IMC plan is complete. The work, however, is not finished. There are ads to be filmed, print ads to be placed, consumer and trade promotions to be distributed, salespeople to contact, and a multitude of additional marketing tasks to finalize. In the end, the evaluation programs you have established should provide valuable information about how well the IMC plan worked. At that point, a new IMC cycle will begin. Good luck!

Appendix

This IMC Pro Booklet can be used with the Clow and Baack textbook: *Integrated Advertising, Promotions, and Marketing Communications*, (3rd edition). This IMC Plan Pro booklet helps you apply theories and learn the concepts presented in the various chapters of the textbook. For each chapter, suggestions are provided that ties the material from the chapter to the IMC Plan Pro Booklet and IMC Plan Pro disk. The Chapter headings refer to the Chapters in the *Integrated Advertising, Promotions, and Marketing Communications* the textbook.

Chapter 1: Pick Your Product

An effective Integrated Marketing Communications program involves applying the concepts and techniques contained in the Clow and Baack textbook. To understand how the process unfolds, your assignment for Chapter One is to pick a product that can be used throughout the entire book. Possible product choices include:

- Individual size bottled water
- New ink pen
- Chopsticks
- Baseball
- Perfume or cologne
- Purse
- Errand running and reminder service
- E-trade service for Nasdaq stocks

While not an actual part of the IMC Campaign, it is beneficial to relate your product to the communications model described in Chapter One

Chapter 1 Exercise: Pick a product.

Chapter 2: Developing a Brand Name and an Image Management Program

In this chapter, you should develop a corporate image and a brand strategy reflecting Sections 3.1 to 3.3 of the IMC Campaign outline. More specifically, a brand name and an accompanying logo should be designed and chosen. Also, a corporate name, which may or may not be the same as the brand name, should be selected.

In Section 3.1, the corporate image to be conveyed to the various publics is specified. You should discuss how to accomplish this. In Section 3.2, the brand name is identified and a logo is developed following the principles presented in the text. Also, a brand strategy should be developed in this section. In Section 3.3, one of the positioning strategies discussed in the textbook should be chosen.

You may have to come back to these sections after you finish Chapter 4 of the textbook, because in Chapter 4 you will learn how to conduct a promotions opportunity analysis. This analysis should help to identify your target market and segmentation analysis. These must fit with your brand strategy and product positioning approach. It is important to integrate the corporate strategy, brand name, logo, and positioning strategy together with the analysis that will is being conducted in Chapter 4

Chapter Exercise: Complete Sections 3.1, 3.2 and 3.3.

Chapter 3: Inducing Consumers and Businesses to Buy a Product

Developing a high quality IMC program requires an understanding of consumer buying behaviors and business-to-business buyer behaviors. Based on the concepts presented in this chapter, you should begin working on section 2.0 of the IMC Campaign. While this section will be completed with Chapter 4, it is a good idea to start working on it in conjunction with the materials from this chapter. The customer analysis, section 2.1.4, is the most relevant section. You should address the consumer decision-making process, or the business-to-business decision making process and how it relates to your products. Analysis of an external information search is especially important here. The information yielded by the search will be used in developing a media plan in later chapters.

In addition to a consumer market, most goods and services have potential business buyers. In addition, most goods, and some services, will have some type of distribution channel to ensure easy access by consumers. You should consider potential business-to-business customers as well as channel members who would purchase the product. Wholesalers, distributors and retailers should be identified. Section 3.4 of the IMC Plan Pro outline deals with the distribution strategy. Section 3.5 examines the business-to-business marketing angle. Discussing the type of good or service being marketed as well as the type of customers who may purchase the product is helpful in understanding and reaching these markets.

Chapter 3 Exercise: Complete Sections 3.4 and 3.5. Begin working on Section 2.0, especially Section 2.1.4.

Chapter 4: Conducting a Promotions Opportunity Analysis for Your Product

This chapter is critical because it lays the foundation for the IMC campaign. If you have not already done so, it is important to conduct a promotions opportunity analysis as discussed in the chapter. The communications market analysis component of the promotional analysis is Section 2.0 of the outline for the IMC campaign. In this analysis, you should examine the:

- Competition
- Opportunities
- Target market(s)
- Customers

The last part of the communications market analysis, the positioning of the product, should have been completed, however it is a good idea to go back and review the information to be sure it matches the opportunity analysis you just completed.

In the first step of the development of the IMC campaign, you should identify competitors and the communication strategies those competitors are using. You should also examine the various target markets for the product to help identify any new opportunities that exist.

The next step is to establish the three communication objectives you wish to accomplish. The first communication objective deals with the consumer market, the second

183

with the channel of distribution, and the third with the business-to-business market. The communication objectives are to be placed in Section 4.1 of the IMC Plan. In later chapters, these communication objectives will be re-evaluated, but at this point you should begin to establish the objectives to be accomplished, based on the communications market analysis.

The next step involves establishing a budget. We would suggest a $200 million communications budget. The breakdown for this budget comes later. At this point you should identify which method will be used in developing the communications budget after the company is fully established. Also, you should utilize the Web site to see if you can find the promotional budget of any of your competitors. This information should be placed in Section 4.2 of the IMC Campaign.

The final component of the IMC campaign studied in this chapter is the market segmentation strategy. Based on their communications market analysis and especially your target market analysis, you should decide the segmentation strategy they will use and which target market(s) you wish to pursue. This is section 2.2 of the IMC Campaign.

Chapter 4 Exercise: Complete Sections 2.1, 2.2, 4.1 and 4.2.

Chapter 5: Constructing an Advertising Program

A critical decision to be made in this chapter is the choice of an outside advertising agency. You should begin by exploring whether or not an outside agency is desirable, of if the work can be performed in-house. You should go through the steps outlined in the chapter in terms of selecting an advertising agency. These materials are to be placed in Section 4.3 of the IMC campaign.

The second part of the IMC Campaign in this Chapter is where you discuss how the IMC budget will be allocated for each communications objective and what portion of that budget will be devoted to advertising. You should take the total IMC Campaign budget of $200 million, or whatever you have decided, and divide it among IMC Objectives One, Two and Three with a rationale for the decision. This information is then written into sections 5.1, 6.1 and 7.1 of the IMC Campaign. Many of you will not have any experience with budgeting; therefore, the following budget breakdown is suggested.

- IMC Objective 1: $ 60 million

- IMC Objective 2: $100 million

- IMC Objective 3: $ 40 million

Objective 2 deal with the distribution channel and trade promotions. Typically, these two elements account for 50% of all marketing dollars spent. Thus, allocating a total of $100 million matches current industry practice. The $60 million for Objective 1 allows for a greater emphasis on the consumer market than the business-to-business market.

The third part of the IMC Campaign assignment for this chapter is to complete Sections 5.2.1.1 and 5.2.1.2 for IMC Objective One, Sections 6.2.1.1 and 6.2.1.2 for IMC Objective Two, and Sections 7.2.1.1 and 7.2.1.2 for IMC Objective Three. Sections 5.2.1.1, 6.2.1.1 and 7.2.1.1 require you to explain how much of each budget will be used for advertising and the goals you wish to accomplish with the advertising. Bear in mind that you will need money for trade promotions, sales promotions, personal selling, sponsorships, direct marketing programs, and all other marketing program that will assist in the accomplishment of each IMC objective. This exercise is to be completed for each IMC objective. In addition to deciding on the budget amount, you should decide on the type of communications budget that will be used in terms of a pulsating, flighting, or continuous approach. You should justify the budgeting method chosen.

The final part of this chapter presents the Creative Brief, which is found in Sections 5.2.1.2, 6.2.1.2 and 7.2.1.2 of the IMC Campaign outline. Following the example used in the text and based upon their promotion opportunity analysis, you should prepare a Creative Brief.

Chapter 6 Exercise: Complete Sections 4.3, 5.1, 5.2.1.1, 5.2.1.2, 6.1, 6.2.1.1., 6.2.1.2, 7.1, 7.2.1.1, and 7.2.1.2.

Chapter 6: Choosing the Correct Appeal for an IMC Advertising Campaign

In this chapter, the first part of the advertising design as it relates to the Creative Brief is considered. The second part of advertising design will be written after Chapter 7 has been analyzed. Both Chapter 6 and 7 are placed in Sections 5.2.1.3, 6.2.1.3, and 7.2.1.3 of the IMC outline.

The three key theories presented in chapter 6 should be utilized in the development of advertisements. These include: the hierarchy of effects model, means-ends theory, and visual and verbal imaging. A means-end chain should be prepared for each creative brief. If prepared properly, the means-end chain should work for any type of media choice and more importantly, guide in the actual development of the advertisement. In addition to discussing the visual and verbal image issues, you should prepare a tagline to be used in all advertisements to create consistency among the various IMC components.

The next part of Sections 5.2.1.3, 6.2.1.3, and 7.2.1.3 is deciding on the type of appeal to be used. The appeal may be different for print ads than for television advertising or billboard ads.

Chapter 7 Exercise: Work on Sections 5.2.1.3, 6.2.1.3 and 7.2.1.3.

Chapter 7: Selecting an Executional Framework for an IMC Advertising Campaign

Chapter 7 is the one most individuals look forward to with the greatest anticipation because it involves preparing the actual advertisements. To get a feel for the challenge in creating an advertisement, you may want to create at least one broadcast ad and one print ad. For broadcast advertisements, you should create a storyboard with 6 to 12 captures. It is important to allocate a budget for the creation of each advertisement.

Before designing the advertisements, think about the various message strategies to employ, including cognitive, affective, and conative. You will need to choose an executional framework format, such as animation, slice of life, testimonial, dramatization, or one of the others. Finally, a spokesperson should be selected for the advertisement. If the spokesperson is a celebrity, the cost of the celebrity endorsement must be considered. Once these decisions are made, you should then create your advertisements. The textbook provides an excellent illustration of the process and factors that should be used in the development of the advertisements as well as helpful hints in evaluating the effectiveness of the ads. All of this information as well as the completed advertisements should be placed in Sections 5.2.1.3, 6.2.1.3, and 7.2.1.3 of the IMC outline.

Chapter 7 Exercise: Complete Sections 5.2.1.3, 6.2.1.3 and 7.2.1.3.

Chapter 8: Selecting Media for an IMC Advertising Campaign

The portions of the IMC Campaign to be completed in this Chapter are 5.3, 6.3, and 7.3. For each target market, media should be chosen that will best reach the market. You should decide how much money will be spent on the media plan after deducting the cost of advertising production.

Once the budget is completed, you should develop a media plan. The plan should be for one year and include the following information:

- Media choice (television, radio, magazine, etc.)
- Program within media (*Scrubs, Nightly News, Desperate Housewives,* etc.)
- The cost per advertisement, number of advertisements, and total cost
- CPM
- Rating points, gross rating points and cost per rating point
- Discussion of frequency and reach

If rating points, audience size, and other data are not available, you should estimate these figures and provide a justification of how you arrived at these estimates. You should prepare tables such as the one illustrated in the chapter. The presentation should include a media plan, especially for the media choice and programs within the media, as well as a rationale for each decision.

In preparing the media plan, consider business-to-business advertising needs as well as advertising that may need to be directed toward individual channel members. This portion of the media plan will undoubtedly look different than the media plan for consumers.

Chapter 8 Exercise: Complete Sections 5.3, 6.3 and 7.3.

Chapter 9: Matching Trade Promotion Tactics with an IMC Advertising Campaign

In this Chapter, you are to examine the trade promotions portion of the IMC Campaign. It is very likely that you will not have any experience with trade promotions. Consequently, it will be difficult to estimate costs and to know the best types of trade promotions for individual products. By this point, you have already identified channel members such as wholesalers, distributors, and retailers. For most products, approximately 50% of the IMC budget will go to trade promotions. It is recommended that only 40% or $80 million be allocated for trade promotions in this assignment.

You should begin by carefully examining the various types of trade promotions presented in the Chapter. If a new product is being introduced, a slotting fee, which can range from $100 to $1000 per store, may be charged. If the product is going to be stocked in discount stores such as Wal-Mart, the slotting fee for just Wal-Mart will range from $280,000 to $2,800,000. To encourage retailers and wholesalers to stock the merchandise, an off-invoice allowance should be offered. Without a strong brand name to pull the product through the channel, this off-invoice allowance encourages channel members to push the product through to retail stores and consumers.

In addition to the trade promotions, you need to design the product's package. You should also consider POP displays and how important the package design is to retailers trying to stock crowded shelves and aisles.

For this chapter, you will complete Sections 6.2.2 of the IMC Campaign. Trade promotions are not part of IMC Objectives One or Three, which deal with consumer markets and business-to-business markets, respectively. Trade promotions are utilized only for pushing the product through the channel of distribution.

Chapter 9 Exercise: Complete Section 6.2.2.

Chapter 10: Creating Consumer Promotions for an IMC Campaign

For this portion of the IMC Campaign, you are to examine the consumer promotions that will be offered. Consumer promotions should be considered for both the consumer markets

(Objective One) and the business-to-business market (Objective Three). From Chapter 10 of your textbook, consumer promotions that fit with advertisements and other elements of the IMC campaign should be chosen.

As part of the IMC Campaign, you should design the actual consumer promotions items to be used, such as coupons or premiums. By creating the actual consumer promotion, think more carefully about how the marketing piece fits with advertisements already created as well as the other IMC components.

In the first section of this chapter's assignment, you should discuss budgets for consumer promotions. The second section is where you decide on a rationale for the various promotional pieces. The third section requires actual samples of the promotions. When these tasks are completed, you should covered Sections 5.2.2 and 7.2.2 of the IMC Campaign outline.

Chapter 10 Exercise: Complete Sections 5.2.2 and 7.2.2.

Chapter 11: Personal Selling and Database Management

Personal selling strategies vary based on the objectives involved. For Objective One, Section 5.2.3, you should address the issues of selling within the retail environment. You should identify the type of retail sales that would be the most appropriate for the product. A discussion of the consumer buying process will help in understanding the role retail salespeople play as well as how the vending firm can offer training or incentives to enhance sales of the product at the retail level.

The major portion of this chapter deals with how the field sales force handles the channel members and business-to-business customers. You should decide which type of selling relationship the sales force should pursue and how it will be attained. It is important to elaborate on each step in the personal selling process as it applies to your firm. Especially important is the discussion of identifying and qualifying prospects.

Regardless of the type of product being sold, developing a data warehouse is essential. You should discuss the types of data to be collected and how the company will build a data warehouse. It is important to identify the objectives and uses for the data. This aids in terms of knowing the data required and if data should be purchased from an outside vendor or developed internally. You should discuss the concept of data mining as it relates to your products as well as how these activities fit into the IMC Campaign. This section of the report is written for Sections 5.2.5.1, 6.2.4.1, and 7.2.5.1 of the IMC outline. As these sections are being completed, it is likely that you will realize that the data needs for the consumer portion of their IMC Campaign are different from the data needs for either business-to-business customers or channel members.

The second component of database management is the development of a direct marketing program. Prepare a direct marketing program that can serve consumers and the business-to-business markets. The first decision to make is the type(s) of direct marketing methods to be used. This information becomes Sections 5.2.5.2, 6.2.4.2, and 7.2.5.2 of the IMC Campaign outline.

Sections 5.2.5.3 and 7.2.5.3 of the IMC Campaign are any permission marketing programs. Permission marketing can be used for either consumers or business-to-business customers. Sections 5.2.5.4 and 7.2.5.4 address any customer loyalty or frequent shopper programs to be offered. Again, both consumer markets and business-to-business markets may include loyalty or frequent shopper type programs.

At the end of this Chapter, you should have completed Sections 5.2.3, 5.2.5, 6.2.3, 6.2.4, 7.2.3, and 7.2.5 of the IMC Campaign outline.

Chapter 11 Exercise: Complete Sections 5.2.3, 5.2.5, 6.2.3, 6.2.4, 7.2.3, and 7.2.5.

Chapter 12: Generating Positive Publicity and Considering Sponsorships

Section 3.6 of the IMC outline addresses the public relations function. Sections 5.2.4 and 7.2.4 address sponsorship and event marketing issues. In Section 3.6 regarding public relations, first identify various stakeholders then discuss the types of messages that will be conveyed to the various stakeholder groups.

Event and sponsorship marketing has increasingly become more popular. Consider how events and sponsorships create synergies between the event or group being sponsored, the consumers who attend, the company, and the products themselves. You should not only decide how much of their budgets will be used for events and sponsorships, but also discuss the objectives to be accomplished. It is important to relate how the event or sponsorship fits into the overall IMC approach. Events and sponsorships for the consumer market are presented in Section 5.2.4 of the IMC outline and in Section 7.2.4 for business-to-business markets.

Chapter 12 Exercise: Complete Sections 3.6, 5.2.4 and 7.2.4.

Chapter 13: Creating Internet Marketing Plans

The Internet is a vital component of any IMC Campaign. In this section, you are asked to design the opening page of a Web site. This can be done in Word, WordPerfect, or any Web design software such as Front Page depending on your backgrounds and skills. Before the Web site is designed, the function of the Web site and how it will be integrated into the IMC Campaign should be addressed. If the Web site will be used for direct purchases by either consumers or businesses, then you must think about the shopping cart and e-commerce incentives that will be used to attract buyers. You need to discuss how the Internet Web site will interface with the IMC Campaign objectives. When complete, this information becomes Section 4.4 of the IMC Campaign outline.

Chapter 13 Exercise: Complete Section 4.4.

Chapter 14: IMC for Small Businesses and Entrepreneurial Ventures

If the IMC Plan is for a small business, then incorporate the concepts provided from this chapter into your plan. This may require going back to sections you have already completed and revising them. Be sure to think about guerilla marketing and lifestyle marketing ideas.

Chapter 15: Evaluating Your IMC Program

This is the final component of the IMC program. Not only will you discuss how to evaluate an IMC Campaign, but this is the time review the entire plan.

The evaluation aspect of the IMC Campaign can be addressed in one of two ways. First, it can be a separate section of the report (Sections 5.4, 6.4, and 7.4). Second, it can be incorporated into each section of the report. If this latter method is used, you will not need to complete Sections 5.4, 6.4, or 7.4. Instead, the last part of each section of 5.2, 6.2, and 7.2 will be the method of evaluation. For example, after discussing advertising, add a Section 5.2.1.4 or the "Evaluation" component. A similar procedure would be used for trade promotions, consumer promotions, and the other elements. Regardless of the method used, you should discuss methods of evaluation for each component of the IMC program. The first factor that should be considered is the level of the evaluation such as short-term, long-term, product-specific, brand, and corporate. Various evaluation techniques are available and consideration should be given not only to a variety of techniques, but to the ones that will provide the most useful evaluation information.

After completing this portion of their IMC Campaign, it is a good opportunity to review the entire plan to ensure is a comprehensive plan that fully integrates all of the various components. If you have not already done so, be sure to go back and complete Section 1.0, which is the executive summary.

Chapter 15 Exercise: Complete Sections 3.7, 5.4, 6.4 and 7.4. Complete Section 1.0 if not already done.

Annotated Outline Showing Chapter Locations

1.0   Executive Summary *(Chapter 15)*

2.0   Promotion Opportunity Analysis *(Chapters 3, 4)*

    2.1   Communications Market Analysis *(Chapter 4)*

        2.1.1   Competitive Analysis *(Chapter 4)*

        2.1.2   Opportunity Analysis *(Chapter 4)*

        2.1.3   Target Market Analysis *(Chapter 4)*

        2.1.4.   Customer Analysis *(Chapters 3, 4)*

    2.2   Market Segmentation Strategy *(Chapter 4)*

3.0   Corporate Strategies *(Chapters 2, 4, 12, 15)*

    3.1   Corporate Image Strategy *(Chapter 2)*

    3.2   Brand Development Strategy *(Chapter 2)*

    3.3   Brand Positioning Strategy *(Chapter 2)*

    3.4   Distribution Strategy *(Chapter 4)*

    3.5   Business-to-Business Strategy *(Chapter 4)*

    3.6   Public Relations Strategy *(Chapter 13)*

    3.7   Evaluation *(Chapter 15)*

4.0   Integrated Marketing Communications Management *(Chapters 4, 5, 13)*

    4.1   IMC Objectives *(Chapter 4)*

    4.2   IMC Budget *(Chapter 4)*

    4.3   Agency Selection *(Chapter 5)*

    4.4   Internet Web site *(Chapter 13)*

5.0   Integrated Marketing Communication Objective One (Consumer)

    5.1   Budget *(Chapter 5)*

    5.2   Integrated Marketing Communication Methodologies

        5.2.1   Advertising *(Chapters 5, 6, 7)*

            5.2.1.1 Advertising Goals and Budget *(Chapter 5)*

            5.2.1.2 Creative Brief *(Chapter 5)*

            5.2.1.3 Advertising Design *(Chapter 6, 7)*

        5.2.2   Consumer Promotions *(Chapter 10)*

5.2.2.1 Budget Allocation *(Chapter 10)*

5.2.2.2 Consumer Promotion Selection *(Chapter 10)*

5.2.2.3 Sample Consumer Promotions *(Chapter 10)*

5.2.3   Personal Selling *(Chapter 11)*

5.2.4   Sponsorship Programs *(Chapter 12)*

5.2.5   Database Programs *(Chapter 11)*

5.2.5.1 Data Warehouse *(Chapter 11)*

5.2.5.2 Direct Marketing *(Chapter 11)*

5.2.5.3 Permission Marketing *(Chapter 11)*

5.2.5.4 Frequent Shopper Program *(Chapter 11)*

5.3   Media Plan *(Chapter 8)*

5.4   Evaluation *(Chapter 15)*

6.0   Integrated Marketing Communication Objective Two (Distribution Channel)

6.1   Budget *(Chapter 5)*

6.2   Integrated Marketing Communication Methodologies

6.2.1   Advertising *(Chapters 5, 6, 7)*

6.2.1.1 Advertising Goals and Budget *(Chapter 5)*

6.2.1.2 Creative Brief *(Chapter 5)*

6.2.1.3 Advertising Design *(Chapters 6, 7)*

6.2.2   Trade Promotions *(Chapter 9)*

6.2.2.1 Budget Allocation *(Chapter 9)*

6.2.2.2 Trade Promotion Selection *(Chapter 9)*

6.2.2.3 Package Design *(Chapter 9)*

6.2.3   Personal Selling *(Chapter 11)*

6.2.4   Database Programs *(Chapter 11)*

6.2.4.1 Data Warehouse *(Chapter 11)*

6.2.4.2 Direct Marketing *(Chapter 11)*

6.3   Media Plan *(Chapter 8)*

6.4   Evaluation *(Chapter 15)*

7.0   Integrated Marketing Communication Objective Three (Business-to-Business)

7.1   Budget *(Chapter 5)*

7.2 Integrated Marketing Communication Methodologies

    7.2.1 Advertising *(Chapters 5, 6, 7)*

        7.2.1.1 Advertising Goals and Budget *(Chapter 5)*

        7.2.1.2 Creative Brief *(Chapter 5)*

        7.2.1.3 Advertising Design *(Chapters 6, 7)*

    7.2.2 Business-to-Business Promotions *(Chapter 10)*

        7.2.2.1 Budget Allocation *(Chapter 10)*

        7.2.2.2 Business-to-Business Promotion Selection *(Chapter 10)*

        7.2.2.3 Sample Business Promotions *(Chapter 10)*

    7.2.3 Personal Selling *(Chapter 11)*

    7.2.4 Sponsorship Programs *(Chapter 12)*

    7.2.5 Database Programs *(Chapter 11)*

        7.2.5.1 Data Warehouse *(Chapter 11)*

        7.2.5.2 Direct Marketing *(Chapter 11)*

        7.2.5.3 Permission Marketing *(Chapter 11)*

        7.2.5.4 Frequent Shopper Program *(Chapter 11)*

7.3 Media Plan *(Chapter 8)*

7.4 Evaluation *(Chapter 15)*